ECHOES UNHEARD

Reflections on the Unseen
from Mediums, Psychologists,
Scientists, Artists, Spiritualists,
Activists and Environmentalists

by

Debra Skelton

Foreword by
Brian S. Robertson & Simon G. James

An Inner Quest Press Publication

Cover Design by S. Robertson
after "Echo and Narcissus" by Waterhouse (1903)

Tellwell Talent
www.tellwell.ca

ISBN
978-0-2288-9359-2 (Hardcover)
978-0-2288-9358-5 (Paperback)
978-0-2288-9360-8 (eBook)

Acknowledgements & Dedication

I gratefully acknowledge the generosity of
Brian Robertson, Simon James,
Terri Woolgar, Debbie Robertson, Louise Dubé,
and the Inner Quest community to whom
this book is affectionately dedicated.

*"The essential quality of the infinite is its subtlety, its intangibility.
This quality is conveyed in the word 'spirit'
whose root meaning is 'wind or breath'. That
which is truly alive is the energy of spirit,
and this is never born and never dies."*
David Bohm

Table of Contents

List of Portraits

Foreword

In *Echoes Unheard,* Debra has once again uncovered the voices of the forgotten. In this sequel to *Echoes: Teachings from the Past, Wisdom for the Present,* we hear from those who share their understanding and experience of Otherness and the outer realms of consciousness - with passion, wit, and humour. At the same time, she amplifies the voices of our modern researchers who bring further insights to our understanding of human and divine consciousness.

Since Debra walked through our doors many years ago, a resolved sceptic brimming with questions and challenges, we have watched her passion unfold for the tradition and philosophy of this esoteric tradition to which we belong, and from which emerged so many of the great social movements of the last two hundred years. With curiosity and wonderment, she embarked upon a complex and often difficult journey that led, among other revelations, to the creation of these books. In the process, she has unearthed ideas, people, and events unknown or, sadly, forgotten altogether.

Echoes Unheard takes us on a voyage through time and awakens us to the rich and fascinating voices of the past interwoven with those of the modern world – all with an enduring relevance to the human experience. Just as Debra's personal journey led to the discovery of her own voice, she, in turn, offers us an appreciation of our own by allowing long silent voices to speak once again. The collective vision of these pioneers, past and present, propels us toward the creation of future echoes, still in the making and as yet unheard.

Brian S. Robertson and Simon G. James
Inner Quest Foundation

Preface

Echoes Unheard is an offering of diverse thoughts on the Unseen world from mediums, psychologists, scientists, artists, spiritualists, activists and environmentalists, past and present, and have been selected for their relevance to the contemporary spiritual seeker.

Chapters One to Five feature aspects of science and spirituality, mediumship, transpersonal and transcendent experience, spiritual development, and socio-economic movement. Chapter Six comprises excerpts from the journals, newspapers and periodicals of the time. Some bear an uncanny ring of familiarity to the pressing issues of our day while others were chosen simply for their sheer curiousness. Still others reflect the prevalent sense of freedom felt by so many at being unshackled from the orthodox religious dogma of the time which, heretofore, had dominated almost every aspect of conduct within western culture. There was ignited a passionate wave of independent thought out of which emerged the significant social reforms of the era - women's suffrage, childhood education, the abolition of slavery, and socio-economic equality, among others.

I have arranged the passages within each chapter in chronological order to give the reader a sense of changing attitudes over time. Occasionally, minimal modifications to the original text have been made in the interests of readability in an attempt to minimize potential stumbling blocks for the contemporary reader. These include substitutions of some challenging archaic words for more modern terms, neutralization of gender assignations when appropriate to inclusiveness, and juxtaposition of thematically related passages from within the source chapter to accommodate the format. I sincerely hope that I have been successful at maintaining the integrity of the authors' intentions.

The passages in this book reflect diverse perspectives on any given subject. They do not necessarily represent the views or opinions of either myself or the Inner Quest Foundation. I offer them simply as points of contemplation and, more importantly, as encouragements to humanitarian action.

Debra Skelton
Victoria, Canada
May 2023

Introduction

Many of us have an unquenchable desire to understand the Unseen, to know the Unknowable. Throughout history, wise minds from all walks of life have shared that very quest and recorded their insights, neither seeking nor achieving recognition. Many have now been forgotten.

In this volume, I am pleased to bring forward some of those unheard voices within the fields of mediumship, psychology, science, art, activism, environmentalism, and spirituality, and to place them in the company of those to whom history was somewhat kinder. Juxtaposed with these are revelations from some of our remarkable contemporary voices, revealing how far we have come and how far we have not.

Just as the medium is a bridge between two states of consciousness, so this book is intended to be a bridge between some long-held perceptions within our mediumistic lineage, and the contemporary investigations of those researchers engaged in seeking the how and why of consciousness. The former bring their immediate experience of other realms to the table, while the latter offer us a wealth of possibilities around the 'hard question'[1] and other aspects of consciousness study.

---

[1] The hard problem of consciousness is the problem of explaining how and why physical processes give rise to subjective conscious experience. Chalmers, D. (1995) *Facing Up to the Problem of Consciousness.* Journal of Consciousness Studies, 2(3), pp. 200–229.

At the Inner Quest Centre, we explore aspects of consciousness through both the mediumistic and the transpersonal lens; that said, we are taking it as read that consciousness is not *generated* by the body but rather that it is *intrinsic to* the body. In this sense, theory and experience merge and blend in an integrated practice within the work that we do.

Bridges themselves are not a destination. However, I hope to encourage a rapprochement between the worlds and, as Professor Brian L. Lancaster proposes, a "harmony of inquiry"[2] by which we may all ultimately benefit.

Those reading this book will likely sense an affinity with the many who sought and who now seek a knowing such as this. If so, may their words inspire you on your own path of discovery, and may your insights be reflected in your action while you are yet in this physical existence.

Debra Skelton

---

[2]   Lancaster, Brian L. (2004). *Approaches to Consciousness: The Marriage of Science and Mysticism*. Red Globe Press.

Portrait Gallery

J. FRANK BAXTER
1841-1904
SINGER, MEDIUM
SPIRITUALIST LECTURER

MARC BEKOFF
1945-
ACTIVIST, AUTHOR
PROFESSOR, ECOLOGY AND
EVOLUTIONARY BIOLOGY
FOUNDER, JANE GOODALL INSTITUTE

HELENA P. BLAVATSKY
1831-1891
CO-FOUNDER,
THEOSOPHICAL SOCIETY

HELEN TEMPLE BRIGHAM
1843-1923
MEDIUM, LECTURER
PASTOR, SPIRITUAL AND ETHICAL SOCIETY

ANNIE BRITTAIN
1880-1969
MEDIUM

EMMA HARDINGE BRITTEN
1823-1899
MEDIUM, LECTURER, AUTHOR
FOUNDING EDITOR, TWO
WORLDS JOURNAL

THOMAS BURNSIDE
DATES UNKNOWN
MEDIUM & JOURNAL CONTRIBUTOR

JOHN CAIRD
1820-1898
THEOLOGIAN
PRINICPAL, UNIVERSITY OF GLASGOW

ALEXANDER CALDER
19TH CENTURY
PSYCHICAL RESEARCHER
PRESIDENT, BRITISH NATIONAL
ASSOCIATION OF SPIRITUALISTS

WILLIAM CROOKES
1832-1919
PHYSICIST, INVENTOR
PRESIDENT, SOCIETY FOR
PSYCHICAL RESEARCH

MICHAEL DANIELS
1950-
AUTHOR, PARAPSYCHOLOGIST
EDITOR, TRANSPERSONAL
PSYCHOLOGY REVIEW

ANDREW JACKSON DAVIS
1826-1910
MEDIUM, AUTHOR, HUMANITARIAN
'FATHER OF MODERN SPIRITUALISM'

VAN BUREN DENSLOW
1834-1902
PROFESSOR OF POLITICAL ECONOMY

ARTHUR CONAN DOYLE
1859-1930
PHYSICIAN, AUTHOR
PSYCHICAL RESEARCHER

HENRY DRUMMOND
1851-1897
BIOLOGIST, LECTURER

ALBERT EINSTEIN
1879-1955
PHYSICIST
PHILOSOPHER, HUMANITARIAN

G. HARTELIUS, G. ROTHE, P. ROY
21ST CENTURY
TRANSPERSONAL PSYCHOLOGISTS

EILEEN GARRETT
1893-1970
MEDIUM, PARAPSYCHOLOGIST

ARTHUR HASTINGS
1935-2014
PSYCHOLOGIST
PROFESSOR, INSTITUTE OF
TRANSPERSONAL PSYCHOLOGY
DIRECTOR, WILLIAM JAMES CENTER

ERIC HATTON
1926-2015
SPEAKER, BROADCASTER
PRESIDENT, SPIRITUALISTS
NATIONAL UNION

THE HAYDENS
19TH CENTURY
MARIA HAYDEN, MEDIUM
WILLIAM HAYDEN, PHYSICIAN

J. ARTHUR HILL
1872-1951
AUTHOR, PARAPSYCHOLOGIST

JAMES HILLMAN
1926-2011
PSYCHOLOGIST, AUTHOR
PHILOSOPHER
DIRECTOR OF STUDIES,
C.G. JUNG INSTITUTE

ERNEST S. HOLMES
1887-1960
TEACHER, AUTHOR
NEW THOUGHT MOVEMENT

JOHN PAGE HOPPS
1834-1911
UNITARIAN & SPIRITUALIST MINISTER
EDITOR, THE TRUTHSEEKER
& DAYBREAK

JAMES H. HYSLOP
1854-1920
PSYCHOLOGIST, PROFESSOR OF ETHICS
FOUNDER, AMERICAN INSTITUTE
FOR SCIENTIFIC RESEARCH

SIMON G. JAMES
1967-
TEACHER, HEALER, MEDIUM
VICE-PRESIDENT, INNER
QUEST FOUNDATION

WILLIAM JAMES
1842-1910
'FATHER OF AMERICAN PSYCHOLOGY'

ROBIN WALL KIMMERER
1953-
PROFESSOR, ENVIRONMENTAL BIOLOGY
FOUNDER, CENTRE FOR NATIVE
PEOPLES AND THE ENVIRONMENT

CARL G. JUNG
1875-1961
PSYCHIATRIST
FOUNDER, PSYCHOANALYTIC
PSYCHOLOGY

BRIAN L. LANCASTER
1951-
EMERITUS PROFESSOR,
TRANSPERSONAL PSYCHOLOGY,
LIVERPOOL JOHN MOORES
UNIVERSITY
HONORARY RESEARCH FELLOW,
CENTRE FOR JEWISH STUDIES,
MANCHESTER UNIVERSITY

GLADYS OSBORNE LEONARD
1882-1968
MEDIUM
SOCIETY FOR PSYCHICAL RESEARCH

OLIVER LODGE
1851-1940
PHYSICIST, INVENTOR
SOCIETY FOR PSYCHICAL RESEARCH

LOUISA LOWE
1820-1901
ACTIVIST
FOUNDER, LUNACY LAW
REFORM ASSOCIATION

FREDERIC W. H. MEYERS
1843-1901
PHILOLOGIST, CLASSICIST
FOUNDER, SOCIETY FOR
PSYCHICAL RESEARCH

J. J. MORSE
1848-1919
MEDIUM, LECTURER
HUMANITARIAN

TERRY PATTEN
1951-2021
AUTHOR, ACTIVIST
ENVIRONMENTALIST

CORAL POLGE
1924-2001
SPIRIT ARTIST & MEDIUM

RAVI RAVINDRA
1939-
PROFESSOR, COMPARATIVE RELIGION,
PHILOSOPHY & PHYSICS

ESTELLE ROBERTS
1889-1970
MEDIUM

BRIAN S. ROBERTSON
1958-
HEALER, TEACHER, MEDIUM
PRESIDENT, INNER QUEST
FOUNDATION

OLIVER ROBINSON
1976-
LECTURER, AUTHOR
PROFESSOR OF PSYCHOLOGY

ENA TWIGG
1914-1984
MEDIUM, HEALER

CHARLES WENTWORTH UPHAM
1802-1875
POLITICIAN
U.S. HOUSE OF REPRESENTATIVES

ALFRED R. WALLACE
1823-1913
ACTIVIST, NATURALIST
PSYCHIC INVESTIGATOR
ANTHROPOLOGIST
BIOLOGIST, GEOGRAPHER

BARONESS ADELMA VAY
1840-1925
MEDIUM, PHILANTHROPIST

RAY WOOLLAM
1927-2021
TEACHER, MINISTER
PHILOSOPHER, AUTHOR, ACTIVIST

CHAPTER ONE

Science and Spirituality

Oliver Lodge
The Wider View 1870

There are some who regard scientific advances with dislike, thinking that the process will be death to mystery and will reduce all nature to the matter-of-fact and commonplace. But those who realize the way in which creation is bound together forming one continuous and infinite whole, will have no such fear.

The work of the delver and digger is of the utmost value; yet they must not think that theirs is the only method of value; or that the work of the humanist, the inspiration of the poet, and the guidance available through intuition are deceitful will-o'-the-wisps which lead to nothing.

Wordsworth strongly denounces the narrowing tendency which specialization may have upon the intelligence if pursued without any wider and more comprehensive view. Scientific men, more than others, should keep their mind and senses open to a broader outlook, and to the reception of all that be discerned in the great amphitheatre of Truth. It is unfortunate when our higher faculties suffer atrophy through over-specialization, or when - due to overly focussed work - our patent of nobility is diminished.

Truth has many channels for entering the mind, and conviction of truths can be attained during moods - not only of active inquiry - but of passive receptively also.

Alfred R. Wallace
Force of Evidence 1870

At least three times within the last twenty-five years I have had to face imminent death. What I felt on these occasions was a gentle melancholy at the thought of quitting this wonderful and beautiful earth, to enter upon a sleep which might know no waking. I knew that the great problem of conscious existence was one beyond man's grasp, and this gave some hope that existence might be independent of the body.

During twelve years of tropical wanderings, occupied in the study of natural history, I had heard occasionally of the strange phenomena said to be occurring in America and Europe under the general names of "table-turning" and "spirit rapping". Being aware that there were mysteries connected with the human mind which modern science ignored because it could not explain them, I determined to seize the first opportunity on my return home to examine into these matters.

I ought to state that, for twenty-five years, I had been an utter sceptic as to the existence of any superhuman intelligences, and I never for a moment contemplated the possibility that such marvels could be literally true. I held an ingrained prejudice against even such a word as 'spirit' which I have hardly yet overcome. I came to the inquiry, therefore, utterly unbiased by hopes or fears, because I knew that my belief could not affect the reality. If I have now changed my opinion, it is simply by the force of evidence.

Intelligent Investigation 1870

The assertion that Spiritualism is a revival of old superstitions is so utterly unfounded as to be hardly worth notice. A science of human nature which is founded on observed facts; which takes no beliefs on trust; which promotes investigation and self-reliance as the first duties of intelligent beings - is the natural enemy of all superstition.

Spiritualism is an experimental science, and affords a sure foundation for a true philosophy and a religion. It abolishes the terms 'supernatural' and 'miracle' and, in doing so, explains whatever is true in the superstitions and so-called miracles. It is able to harmonise conflicting creeds and it must ultimately lead to concord among mankind in the matter of religion, which has for so many ages been the source of unceasing discord and incalculable evil; and it will be able to do this because it appeals to evidence instead of faith, and substitutes facts for opinions. It is thus able to demonstrate the source of much of the teaching that men have so often held to be divine.

Van Buren Denslow
Value of Scepticism 1878

Spirituality is a necessary force in civilization, but it never includes all truths, nor all duty. It needs the antagonism of a vigorous scientific and philosophic scepticism to prevent it from running civilization down into ecclesiastical bondage and barbarism, as illustrated by the great religious crimes, wars, and persecutions. Religion needs to be antagonized by a powerful philosophical scepticism in order to express, by the joint operation of the two opposing forces, the whole truth, and the whole duty of man.

Henry Drummond
The Natural Law of Continuity 1888

The Law of Continuity says that if Nature be a harmony, then mankind - physical, mental, moral, and spiritual – is included within its circle. It is altogether unlikely that the spiritual human being should be separated from the physical human being. It is indeed difficult to conceive that one set of principles should guide natural life, and these suddenly give way to another set of principles, altogether unrelated, when applied to spiritual life. Humankind cannot be separated into two such incoherent halves.

While there are many harmonies, there is but one Harmony. The breaking up of the phenomena of the universe into groups, and the allocation of certain laws to each, are artificial. We find an evolution in botany, another in geology, and another in astronomy, and the effect is to lead one to look upon these three as distinct evolutions. But these sciences are mere departments created by ourselves to facilitate knowledge - reductions of Nature to accommodate the scale of our own intelligence. And we must beware of breaking up nature, except for the purpose of study. We must keep ourselves in practice by constantly thinking of Nature as a whole.

J. Arthur Hill
An Illusion of Separateness 1918

We belong to a material universe; our bodies are part of the earth's substance. It is reasonable to believe that on the inner or spiritual side, we are in connection with a larger Being. At this point, however, we run into the philosophical problem of the One and the Many. We know ourselves as separate entities here, yet we believe that in the Divine we live and move and have our being. No doubt this looks like inconsistency, an acceptance of two incompatibles.

But our separateness is an illusion. My finger and thumb are separate things, and they press in opposing directions as I hold the pen with which I am writing: but they are unified in the higher synthesis of the hand; the apparent separateness and opposition are needed in the furtherance of purposes which they do not themselves understand. Similarly, it is reasonable to believe that, by the strivings and oppositions of our individual spirits, some higher purpose is being achieved. What that purpose is, I do not, and cannot know; nor what the Being is whose will and purpose direct our petty activities. These matters transcend my faculties, and I will not pretend to know when I am well aware that I do not know.

But the belief is a rational one. And when it is it attained, the question of personal survival becomes unimportant. It becomes a sort of side issue, a temporary crutch, until we reach the mountaintop and can see the wider vision. The task is as religious as it is secular; for Science and Philosophy are only laborious efforts to learn as much as may be of the mind of God.

A Balanced View 1918

I am a member of the Society for Psychical Research, which investigates psychic phenomena in a careful scientific way, and I'm always glad to be informed of any experiences which come within the range of our studies. I keep an open mind. But the subject is so comparatively new, and is so beset with difficulties, that I am sure it is much too early to come to any definite conclusions. Therefore, I content myself with studying the evidence, and applying thereto certain "working hypotheses" which can be modified or replaced by better ones, if further facts should require it.

I include survival of personality and possible communications from surviving minds, among these working hypotheses; not because I want to, but because I cannot honestly avoid it. For, as it seems to me, there is no other hypothesis that even comes near to being reasonable and scientific with regard to some of the phenomena which my friends and I have witnessed and recorded. I may say also that I prefer people to err on the side of scepticism rather than on the side of belief. We want no return of witch-manias. We want cool, balanced judgment, with an earnest desire for the truth, and plenty of patience in the seeking of it. "What mankind at large mostly lacks" says the late Professor William James, "is criticism and caution, not faith."

Real in the Unseen 1918

Truth has to be re-stated in every period of time, in the new language, and harmonious with new facts, outer and inner. Science is discovering the spiritual world which it temporarily denied through short-sighted concentration on the material aspect of things. It is now learning that the Real is in the Unseen.

Albert Einstein
Mystery 1931

The most beautiful experience we can have is the mysterious. It is the fundamental emotion which stands at the cradle of true art and true science. Whoever does not know it and can no longer wonder, no longer marvel, is as good as dead, and his eyes are dimmed. It was the experience of mystery - even if mixed with fear - that engendered religion. A knowledge of the existence of something we cannot penetrate, perceptions of the profoundest reason and the most radiant beauty which only in their most primitive forms are accessible to our minds - it is this knowledge and this emotion that constitute true religiosity; in this sense, and in this alone, I am a deeply religious man.

I cannot conceive of a God who rewards and punishes his creatures, or has a will of the kind that we experience in ourselves. I am satisfied with the mystery of the eternity of life, and with the awareness or a glimpse of the marvellous structure of the existing world, and of the Reason that manifests itself in nature.

Perception of the Divine 1934

To the naïve, God is a being from whose care one hopes to benefit and whose punishment one fears, similar to that of a child for its father, a being to whom one stands, so to speak, in a personal relation however deeply it may be tinged with awe.

But the scientist is possessed by the sense of universal causation. Their spirituality takes the form of a rapturous amazement at the harmony of natural law which reveals an intelligence of such superiority that, compared with it, all the systematic thinking and acting of human beings is an utterly insignificant reflection. This feeling is the guiding principle of their life and work (insofar as they succeed in keeping themselves from the shackles of selfish desire).

It is, beyond question, closely akin to that which has possessed the spiritual geniuses of all ages.

In their struggle for the ethical good, teachers of religion must have the stature to give up the doctrine of a personal God; that is, give up that source of fear and hope which in the past placed such vast power in the hands of priests. In their labours they will have to avail themselves of those forces which are capable of cultivating the Good, the True, and the Beautiful in humanity itself. This is, to be sure, a more difficult but an incomparably more worthy task.

Ravi Ravindra
Sacred Significance 1995

When the intellect is not oriented towards and in the service of Divine wisdom, it is bound to become a force for fragmentation... Science has been, for some of the greatest scientists, a spiritual path, a way to connect with and serve the Sacred. Rightly understood and oriented, it can be so again. The best of the scientists have always approached science as a sacred activity - an activity that could yield the secrets of the 'Old One' (Einstein). "Every scientist is potentially a priest of God in the temple of Nature." [3]

For Einstein, as for so many great scientists, the Sacred was not discovered or proved by their science. The Sacred called them, pervaded their lives and gave significance to their scientific activity - as it would have to their other activities such as music or poetry or painting, if they had been called to celebrate the Sacred through these, as had been Bach, Kalidas and El Greco. Could we then say that religion without scientific knowledge is ineffective, but science without religious perception is insignificant?

Power Without Wisdom 1995

There is a sense in some circles of an erosion of values and of meaning in human life which is associated with the rapid

---

[3]   Kepler, Johannes. (1987). *Science and the Sacred*. The Encyclopedia of Religion, eds. M. Eliade, el. al.; Macmillan Publishing Co.

industrialization brought about by the developments in science and technology. These attitudes and concerns about the promise as well as the threat of science and technology are felt by thoughtful and sensitive people everywhere, but even more strongly in non-Western traditional societies. Are their traditional modes of knowing - some of which have long histories and outstanding practical applications especially in the areas of physical and emotional healing, and family and social relationships - simply going to be marginalized by modern science and technology? Military and industrial power depend on science and technology, and no one wishes to be without power. But from the point of view of some of the leaders of traditional cultures, Western societies have won these powers at the cost of spiritual and human values, acquiring power without wisdom and compassion.

A recovery of the spiritual values inherent in the practice of science, even though overshadowed by many internal and external forces, would help heal our modern world in which science plays such a crucial and vital role, both in the West as well as in the East.

Marc Bekoff
Science of Spirit and Compassion 2000

Historically, scientists were placed on pedestals by non-scientists (and by scientists themselves). People who questioned science were anti-intellectual, perhaps Luddites, and summarily dismissed. After all, scientists continually discover innumerable ways to make our lives longer and presumably better. But I think it can do better...traditional reductionistic science often falls short because it fragments the world. Reductionistic science disembodies and dissects wholes into parts.

I believe holistic and heart-driven science is needed, deep science that is impregnated with spirit and compassion. Holistic, heartfelt science reinforces a sense of togetherness in which the seer and seen are one. It fosters the development of deep and reciprocal relationships among humans, other animals, and other nature, softening our tendencies to control and manage almost everything in sight. Narrow claims that there is only one way to do 'good' science need to be resisted. Allowing individual idiosyncrasies and visions, interdisciplinary collaborations, holism, feeling, and heart to inspire science will make it more exciting and far more likely to be successful. Questioning science and deepening and broadening its scope are healthy moves toward a world in which magnificent nature - her deep and rich sensuality, her beneficence, her complexity - will be respected, cherished, and loved. As a result, we will resonate more as a friend and less as a foe, as we reconcile with the dazzling natural world of which we're an integral part.

Brian L. Lancaster
Harmony of Inquiry 2004

Consciousness is the inner citadel; the essence of what it is to be human. We know it from the inside; or, rather, it is the quality of knowing itself. Here lies the common ground with mysticism, for none have charted the territory of the phenomena of mind more richly than those who walked the path of mysticism. The mystical knowing of God has been identified with knowing the roots of thought and consciousness. And, in relation to non-theistic forms of mysticism, enlightenment is equated with the glowing transparency of a mind that is fully known to itself. In both cases, insight into consciousness has been integral to the path of perfection.

The challenge to understand consciousness demands a harmony of inquiry between science and mysticism. Subtle features of the mind, unnoticed except by the mystic who has been schooled in the distinctive methods of their path, may provide the key for interpreting data thrown up by the relevant sciences. Such mystical insights might enable a richer comprehension of neurophysiological analyses of brain function, or of data from cognitive science concerning perception and memory, for example. And, in complementary fashion, these scientific data can enrich the spiritual quest to explore consciousness inwardly.

Sacred Sciences of the Soul 2004

The challenge of consciousness studies is not simply that of gathering more data on the subject. Rather, it is the challenge to move beyond our compartmentalized scheme of things in order that society might re-balance its sense of values. Again, I think it appropriate to turn the classical question around. We should be asking, not whether consciousness studies is a legitimate discipline, but what is it about ourselves and our society that makes this discipline legitimate for us today.

Essentially, we are experiencing an archetypal shift in perspective, a re-organizing of the *zeitgeist,* which necessitates a re-valuing of the spiritual. Not only is the spiritual becoming an increasingly important source of meaning for many who are no longer nourished through traditional religions, it is also entering the discourse of knowledge, with a significant upsurge of interest in the dialogue between science and spirituality/religion. It might be more accurate to state that spiritual ideas are *re-entering* the discourse of knowledge, for the shift to which I refer takes us back to the heyday of the sacred sciences of the soul, as they were last in evidence during the Renaissance.

Twin Paths to Knowledge 2004

All current theories of consciousness entail a leap of faith. Each has its particular strengths and weaknesses. Physicalist positions have the strength that no reality is posited [advanced] other than that which we can subject to the rigours of scientific examination. But they cannot do more than proffer the hope that some kind of scientific breakthrough will eventually provide us with the full story of consciousness. Theirs is a faith in the power of science. Given the necessity of a leap of faith in addressing the mystery of consciousness, we must ask whether this is the kind of leap for which our culture is searching. Each will have their own answer, but my own sense is that terms such as 'purpose' and 'meaning' are key features of the quest, and that many seek a spiritually satisfying understanding of consciousness. The theory which I have presented in this book[4] meets the challenge by integrating the twin paths to knowledge that dignify human purpose, those of science and religious mysticism.

Oliver Robinson
Do Science and Spirituality Mix? 2017

In considering science and spirituality, certain key commonalties provide the foundation for harmony. Firstly, both science and spirituality are transformative and active ways of knowing through experience. Science pursues truth through its methodology that links the collection of external evidence with mathematics and recent thinking. The intention in the scientific method is to elicit dispassionate and objective knowledge about the external world, which transcends any individual point of view and is superior to common sense. Spirituality perceives truth not as something beyond subjective consciousness, but as a state of awakeness and higher awareness within it. Through practice, the seeker connects with the "ground of being" beyond ego, which is felt to be a source of authentic love, compassion, and peace, that connects people and other living beings together. It is as though we are all cups of ocean and ocean water, and through spiritual practice, we eventually realize our true density as ocean, not cup.

A second key commonality is that both science and spirituality entail reflective questioning, criticality, and a wariness of dogma. Within science, critical thinking is highly valued, and all research is scrutinized...Mature spiritual questioning entails reflecting on whether what is being experienced or learned via one's practice

---

4   Lancaster, Brian L. (2004). *Approaches to Consciousness: The Marriage of Science and Mysticism*. Red Globe Press.

is congruent with reason and intuition, and helpful to personal and social development.

Gould[5] proposes that science and religion cannot mix. He uses the analogy of oil and water to visualize this – if oil and water are put in a jar, they create two distinct layers and don't mix even at the join. That, says Gould, is how religion and science are. In contrast, I propose that science and spirituality definitely *do* mix and overlap. There are scientific approaches to spirituality and spiritual approaches to science, and this interface area between the two is a fascinating and controversial area that I look at in various ways across the chapters of this book.[6]

---

[5] Gould, S. J. (1999). *Rocks of Ages: Science and Religion in the Fullness of Life*. London: Jonathan Cape.

[6] Robinson, Oliver. (2017). *Paths Between Head and Heart*. John Hunt Publishing Ltd.

CHAPTER TWO

Ethical Mediumship

Emma Hardinge Britten
Mediumistic Development 1875

It is our incumbent duty, even an urgent necessity, to preserve the high privileges of spiritual intercourse by studying its laws, and endeavouring scientifically to master its methods, so as to control the communion and be able to conduct it at will.

On this point, remember that all the 'magical arts' are as open to mankind today as ever they were. Whether it be morally proper to seek them or not, is not the question here. We simply reiterate that they are attainable, and with the lights of science we now enjoy, especially in our improved knowledge of psychological and physiological laws, they can be achieved.

The failures of modern mediumistic practice, its degradation, lack of organic power, evil repute, and gradual but sure decadence, all proceed from the human side of the movement. It may be difficult, perhaps impossible, to repair the errors committed, but it is for us to lay the foundation of improved conditions by dealing with the upcoming generation. For this purpose, the wisest course we can now pursue in the interests of truth and posterity, would be to found a new School of the Prophets.

Louisa Lowe
Freedom from Bondage 1877

Our present task is to assure unto mediumship free and fearless exercise, safe alike from prosecutions in the law courts and persecutions in the madhouses. In attacking the very poorest of our brethren (so long as they be honest, disinterested, and true) they are attacking us all. There is not one among us who would not go to prison, and, if need be, to death; in vindication of free thought, unconventionality, and boundless toleration. Let us press onward to its legitimate outcome of universal unity.

Personally, I lean to the opinion that the time has come at last when, emancipated from the child's servitude to ecclesiastical bondage, we are to walk with adult liberty and, with head erect, exchange command for companionship and counsel.

One Drop 1877

To many it has been given to see, in the marvellous manifestations of occult intelligence, proof of the continued existence of those that they have loved and lost, and the firm assurance of their own individual immortality. To me, these manifestations have brought no such conviction.

I can only find in them proof that some intelligence or intelligences do exist and act apart from ordinary matter, and that all intelligences confined in mortal bodies will survive separation from them; but whether as separate entities, or as part of one greater intelligent aggregate, I know not—almost, I add, could care not. Whether our future is to be one of individuality akin to that on earth, or whether the spirit that is in us shall, when severed from the body, merge itself into some great life ocean, one cannot be sure. But it is our duty and our joy to live and labour so that the tiny drop may depart from us purer and nobler than we received it.

Anonymous
Mediumship and Morality 1880

Some seem to suppose that a person endowed with mediumistic ability must possess a superabundance of moral qualities and a more-than-ordinary share of virtues and graces. However, moral qualities are not necessarily associated with the ability to think, speak, be successful in business, or invent; neither are they bound to appear in the character of a medium, no matter how perfect the mediumship may be. Any person may be skilful in their profession and yet be woefully destitute of all moral rectitude.

Now and again the spiritualistic world may be startled with news of the imprudent behaviour of a leading, recognised medium, and then doubts arise as to the genuineness of the manifestations of the suspected medium. It generally ends with those persons declining to place any more reliance on the utterances of that medium. This is a grave mistake. We have known persons to be most reliable mediums but who were lacking in personal honour and integrity. This painful inconsistency shocked us at first. It was only after much earnest thought that we were able to separate the mediumistic qualifications from the moral sentiments.

A medium is an instrument for the transmission of thought from one stage of existence to another; and the faculty to transmit thought depends upon a personal constitution that will readily co-operate and assimilate the thoughts of others. Mediumship is, therefore, a physiological development in precisely the same way that one is constituted with the qualities and abilities of a speaker or an author, or with the ability to invent machinery.

To all our friends, then, we would say, look at the mediumistic qualities independently of moral or intellectual faculties. But, if these higher unfoldments are also found in the medium, so much the better for the mediumship.

James H. Hyslop
Supernormality Not a Test of Truth 1900

Let's say my father dies. An alleged medium says that my father appeared to him and gave his philosophy of the universe. However, my father's opinion after death may not be any better than it was before death. The truth of his opinion must be tested with the same criteria after death as before it, and these criteria are those which we use in science. Revelations are none the better for coming from spirits.

Philosophic systems must be tested by the same standards that prevail with the living. Their origin is one thing, but their validity another question. Indeed we might even be able to prove that a message was false and yet it was a communication from a spirit. Its falsity would not negate the truth of its origin, nor its accuracy support it. The condition of proving its source is one thing, the condition of proving its validity is another. Supernormality is not a test of truth.

I have stated these facts in order to have on record the principles on which psychic research must proceed. The first is the origin of a statement, the question whether it issues from the mind of the medium or transcends it; and the second is whether it is true or not. The solution of the first problem is no assurance that the second is evidence of the validity of the message. It only assures us that we have found some thing besides the mind of the medium as the cause, and the truth remains to be decided by other standards. These facts should always be kept in mind.

Arthur Conan Doyle
Phenomena: What does it Mean? 1918

Are we to satisfy ourselves by simply observing spirit phenomena with no attention to what the phenomena mean, as a remote tribe of indigenous peoples might stare at a wireless telegraph with no comprehension of the messages coming through it? Or shall we construct from the phenomena a paradigm founded upon human reason on the one hand, and upon spiritual inspiration on the other?

These phenomena are beyond being a parlour game or scientific novelty; they are, or should be, taking shape as the foundations of a system of spiritual thought, in some ways confirmatory of ancient systems, in some ways entirely new.

Above all, read the literature on this subject. It has been far too much neglected. Make yourself familiar with the overpowering evidence. Get away from the phenomenal side and learn the philosophy and teachings. There is a whole library of such a literature - of unequal value it is true, but of a high average. Broaden and spiritualize your thoughts. Show the results in your lives. Unselfishness, that is the keynote to progress.

A Sacred Act 1918

There remains the question which troubles many earnest souls as to whether communion with spirit is right. Personally I am not aware of any human power which has been given us without our having the right to use it. On the other hand, I know of no human power which may not be abused. It is an abuse of such a power when it is used in the spirit of mere curiosity. It can be either an absurd farce or the most solemn and sacred of functions.

William Crookes
Imposters[7]

Some so-called mediums of whom the public have heard much are errant imposters who have taken advantage of the public demand for spiritualistic excitement to fill their purses with easily earned cash; while others, who have no monetary motive, are tempted to cheat it would seem, solely by the desire for fame. A first-time inquirer, finding one such case during their first seance,

---

[7]   Published after death. Crookes, William. (1926). *Researches in the Phenomena of Spiritualism*. The Two Worlds Publishing Company, Ltd.

is disgusted with what they detect to be an imposture. They not unnaturally give vent in a sweeping denunciation of mediumship.

There is a wide difference between the tricks of such a physical medium (surrounded by his apparatus and aided by any number of assistants) and the phenomena occurring in the presence of Mr. D.D. Home. These take place in the light, in a private room which, almost up to the commencement of the séance, has been occupied as a living room; and surrounded by those who will not tolerate the slightest deception. Mr. Home has frequently been searched before and after the seances, and he always offers to allow it. During the most remarkable occurrences, I have occasionally held both his hands, and placed my feet on his feet. At no time did I propose a safeguard (for the purpose of rendering trickery less possible) which he did not at once consent to and, frequently, he himself has drawn attention to tests which might be tried.

Gladys Osborne Leonard
Hope 1937

Let us not disdain anything which gives us hope simply because it arises from a source outside our own personal experience. I feel convinced that the scientific acceptance of the existence of the etheric body is very near at hand. The evidence is piling up continually from unimpeachable sources and can no longer be ignored. If, by knowing it to be true, we can bind up broken hearts and give courage to the hopeless, surely such knowledge is well worthwhile. Nothing, not even the certainty of life beyond the grave, will entirely compensate for the actual loss of the physical body of the one we love.

Might we not lose some spiritual quality if we succeeded in obliterating the ability to feel pain or sorrow? There is no great virtue in stoicism, but there is sacredness in tears if they are the evidence of deep love. If we can pass through a great affliction solemnly and slowly, we shall gain inward wisdom beyond the scope of those who endeavour to thrust the painful side of life into oblivion.

Eileen Garrett
Our Inner Faculties 1943

Is super-sensory perception religious in its character? In a certain sense, I believe it is. If religion means "to bind back to the source", the capacity for perception beyond the physical reach of the senses is a phase in the process of that return. It is to be noted that such psychic exercises are in themselves without dogma or denomination. They belong to the great body of natural religion in which all the changing processes of nature are continuously involved.

There are vast areas of potential evolution open to the individual life. Actually, this is all that any one of us needs to realize. From the point of that realization, we can proceed with our own development, if we will. And I have no doubt that, at some stage in our progress, we shall experience capacities of perception which transcend the sensory field.

Naturally, I do not mean to urge anyone to undertake the development of psychic powers. But I do urge many to a serious consideration of those inner faculties which operate beyond the fields of sensory perception. Specifically, I wish to emphasize the fact that what we now speak of as the 'psychic' phases of our human experience are not abnormal, but normal.

Goodbye to Guides[8] *c.1937*

As for 'controls', I myself am about to get rid of them. I have come to the conclusion that the controls of any medium are superficial. I've come to the conclusion that the future proof of mediumship lies in the hands of you and me, and all of us. I think

---

8   Found in Gibbes, E. B. (1937). *Controls as Separate Entities.* Psychic Science; Quarterly Transactions of the British College of Psychic Science, Ltd.

that controls are secondary personalities. I think the sooner we dispose of them and do our own work, the better. I have had my controls examined; and I have now asked St. Thomas Hospital to examine them yet again from the physiological point of view, because I frankly do not believe in them.

I regret that many of our high-priced trance mediums have commercialised this art. Because of that, I repudiate controls and I live for the day when the medium can be and do everything that the control takes upon itself. So let the future of mediumship be in the conscious perceptivity of the medium. I commend that to all of you, because I intend to endorse it in the future.

The Sense and Nonsense of Prophecy 1950

The public is a rather droll lot. On the one hand, they're hard-boiled enough to snort at anything they cannot see or hear. On the other hand, they are gullible enough to patronize the fortune-tellers that infest our cities. The public spends large sums of money to listen to such astounding revelations as, "you're a good friend but a dangerous enemy" or "Wednesday the 16th is an excellent day for personal relationships"; and yet they scorn the serious workers who are trying to throw light on the darker areas inhabited by the human psyche.

One doesn't have to be a profound psychologist to understand this peculiar paradox. When Smith goes to see a fortune-teller and pays his or her dollar, the seer talks exclusively about Smith for a full half hour. Smith believes in the fortune-teller because the fortune-teller tells him or her what he or she wants to hear. Smith probably never heard of the American Society for Psychical Research, but if even so, Smith would undoubtedly regard them as a stuffy group of eccentrics, while old Madame Zoola and her miraculous talking bird (usually a badly feathered canary) is a genius overflowing with amazing gifts, talent, and wisdom!

A Danger and a Blessing 1950

Once upon a time, the knowledge that men sought was available only to the few. Today science has unlocked the doors of the unseen, and the many flock where once only a few were allowed. This opened up new avenues of knowledge to all. This is both a danger and a blessing. The greater the field of knowledge, the greater is the responsibility of all of us.

In the present mechanistic age of instruction, without basic education of a philosophic nature, everyone is obsessed with the idea that he must get to the top in a hurry. Hard work is regarded as a fool's game. The tortoise's approach is outmoded. Why stop to accumulate the basic know-how coupled with reason when the sage of Aquarius, all the way from Atlantis with complete understanding of past and present, offers to unveil your whole future for as little as a dollar?

And that brings me to the theme which was in the back of my mind when I began to write. It is summed up in the word 'responsibility'. I say to all psychic workers: the truth you are dealing with is not for profit or gain; neither is it a fit game to while away the idle moments between lunch and the cocktail hour – it is the unknown power that is related to all things in nature, and that commands the destiny of all mankind.

Carl G. Jung
Discovering Spiritualism[9]

At the end of my second semester, I made another discovery which was to have great consequences. In the library of a classmate's father, I came upon a small book on spiritualistic phenomenon dating from the 1870s. It was an account of the beginnings of Spiritualism and was written by a theologian. My initial doubts were quickly dissipated, for I could not help seeing that the phenomena described in the book were, in principle,

---

[9]   Published after death. Jung, C. G. (1965). *Memories, Dreams, Reflections.* Vintage Books.

much the same as the stories I had heard again and again since my earliest childhood in the country. The material, without a doubt, was authentic. But the great question of whether these stories were physically true was not answered to my satisfaction.

The observations of the Spiritualists, weird and questionable as they seemed to me, were the first accounts I had seen of objective psychic phenomena. Names like Zoellner and Crookes impressed themselves on me, and I read virtually the whole of the literature available to me at the time. Naturally, I also spoke of these matters to my comrades who, to my great astonishment, reacted with derision and disbelief. I wondered at the sureness with which they could assert that things like ghosts and table-turning were impossible and therefore fraudulent, and on the other hand at the evidently anxious nature of their defensiveness. I, too, was not certain of the absolute reliability of the reports but why, after all, should there not be ghosts? How did we know that something was impossible? And above all, what did their anxiety signify? For myself, I found such possibilities extremely interesting and attractive. They added another dimension to my life; the world gained depth and background.

My stepfather sympathized wholeheartedly with my enthusiasm, but everyone else I knew was distinctly discouraging. To this point, I had encountered only the brick wall of traditional views, but now I came up against the steel of people's prejudice, and their utter incapacity to admit unconventional possibilities. I found this even with my closest friends. To them all this was far worse than my preoccupation with theology! I had the feeling that I had pushed to the brink of the world; what was of burning interest to me was null and void for others - even a cause for dread.

Dread of what? I could find no explanation for this. After all, there was nothing preposterous or world-shaking in the idea that there might be events which overstep the limited capacities of space, time, and causality. Animals were known to sense earthquakes beforehand; there were dreams which foresaw the death of certain persons, clocks which stopped the moment of death, glasses which shattered at the critical moment. All these things have been taken for granted in the world of my childhood. And now I was apparently the only person who had ever heard of them. In all earnestness, I asked myself what kind of world I had stumbled into. Plainly the urban world knew nothing about the country world, the real world of mountains, woods, and rivers, of animals and God's thoughts – the plants, and crystals.

I found this explanation comforting. At all events, it bolstered my self-esteem for I realized that, for all its wealth of learning, the urban world was mentally rather limited. This insight proved dangerous because it tricked me into fits of superiority, misplaced criticism, and aggressiveness which got me deservedly disliked. This eventually brought back all the old doubts, inferiority feelings, and depressions – a vicious circle I was resolved to break at all costs. But no longer would I stand outside the world, enjoying the dubious reputation of a freak.

Ena Twigg
Purpose of Mediumship 1973

What are we proving through mediumship? The survival of the individual after death? Certainly. But the implications of that fact are staggering and should affect every facet of living. We try to stand the bereaved on their feet and say, "Go on and use this knowledge." I do not let people use mediumship as a prop; it must be a challenge. There are a number of people I see about once a year who sit as a matter of courtesy to the Other Side. We at least give the other side an opportunity to talk to us. But the sitters are not dependent.

People try to tie mediums to the wheel of continual evidence. It is essential that people receive evidence, but after that there is a whole wealth of information about many subjects that can be gained by using mediumship at other levels.

The purpose of communication is to give people an idea of their true identity and the true purpose of living.

Preoccupation with Phenomena 1973

I know many people who are fascinated with psychic phenomena, but I would caution them to avoid those trifling and sometimes absurd ways of making contact which are extremely dangerous. Do not be misled or too preoccupied with psychic phenomena. They are only important if they lead you to spiritual searching and growth. We are spirit, mind, and body - in that order and not the reverse - and it is the spirit that is the essence that will live on.

There is a beautiful old saying that says, "God breathed out, and man was created. God breathed in, and man began his journey back to his source."

Eric Hatton
That Elusive Something 2010

After six decades of searching and witnessing so many remarkable events, I am still unsure of my true purpose in life. Whilst applauding – and I always will – the importance of such noble work as mediumship, as I grow older I ask myself the question, what was the most important aspect of the many avenues of spirit I have explored?

Please do not misunderstand me, I can never deny or change the wondrous things I've experienced, for some were almost beyond my comprehension…yet my soul cries out for that elusive something which is deeper than anything I can comprehend. Is it that, in realizing my relationship with all God's creation, I have the hunger of the universal mystic, wanting things to be defined yet sensing within me that there are many aspects of my 'destiny' which urge me to continue the journey? For I acknowledge, as do many other searchers, that life both here and in the next phases of the eternal world is but a part of the glorious reality. You must judge for yourselves where you stand in this particular moment of time, but I hope with all my heart that you will find fulfilment.

Brian S. Robertson & Simon G. James
The Whole Point 2017

The whole point of phenomena is to wake us up to the presence of the One, to the mystical nature of life, and to stimulate our own divine nature into action for the benefit of our soul's expression. The ability to move a table around the room is all well and good, but to move a soul toward its fulfilment is the work of the Creator. It is important for those within the mediumistic consciousness to understand that, in this, we are more than magicians. Hopefully we may come to realise that we are God-centred and, with that, are responsible for the spiritual implications of our ability.

Brian S. Robertson
Understanding Mediumship 2022

Mediumship has historically stood outside the western world's predominantly Christian socio-religious structure by virtue of the fact that it is not entirely understood, even by mediums themselves. Mediums are considered to be those who report having contact with the deceased regularly, reliably, and on-demand and who share the specific resulting messages with living people called sitters during an event called a reading.[10] In my experience, however, a medium is more accurately described as someone who has had experiences, either spontaneous or induced, with Other. Otherness implies separateness between self and the divine realms and may refer to other beings or to the Creator.

One approach in which self-conscious awareness is integrated with a sense of spiritual connection is transpersonal psychology. It is a blend of the transcendent and the immanent, an effort to

---

[10]   Beischel, J., Mosher, M., & Boccuzzi, M. (2017). *Quantitative and Qualitative Analyses of Mediumistic and Psychic Experiences*. Threshold: Journal of Interdisciplinary Consciousness Studies.

"understand the cosmos in ways that are not constrained by either the sometimes-heavy hand of religious tradition or the objectifying eye of science…one in which both human science and human spirituality can be honoured."[11]

When we view the scope and application of mediumship within the transpersonal framework, we move away from the confined notion of mediumship as an entertaining spectacle performed by so-called 'gifted' individuals. Rather, we rediscover its potential transpersonal impact in our contemporary world as a healing art which manifests through many people from many walks of life - in an infinite variety of ways.

Simon G. James
Mediumship: A Healing Art 2022

As a researcher and practicing medium, I encourage a reconceptualization of the *mediumistic experience as process,* rooted in - but not enslaved by - verifiable evidence of the survival of consciousness. I believe it may be timely to take a more mature view of mediumship that is less dependent upon material proof and more willing to embrace some empirical uncertainty in order that humanity may reap the benefits of a healing experience, especially those who have suffered great loss. In this way, we might move away from the perception of mediumship as a supernatural oddity and move it into the arena of a universally accepted healing art.

---

[11] Hartelius, G., Rothe, G., & Roy, P. (2013). *Brand for the Burning.* In H. L. Friedman & G. Hartelius (Eds.), The Wiley-Blackwell Handbook of Transpersonal Psychology, Wiley Blackwell.

CHAPTER THREE

Transpersonal & Transcendent Experience

· Andrew Jackson Davis
Affinities 1850

The human soul is constructed upon musical principles which give it an organic tendency toward harmony. Its tones respond to Self-love, Conjugal-love, Parental love, Familial love, and Universal love. But what I desire to impress here is that these Loves are innate affinities which draw soul to soul, and which cause the human mind to feel attracted to corresponding affinities in other minds without reference to time, space, age, position, education or circumstances.

The Spirit World is not far off; it is very near and that which was truly joined here is not separated there. Death does not divide. Loves are responded to by corresponding loves; and thus there proceeds to us a vast variety of good impulses from some of our natural earthly or spiritual affinities.

No Special Favours 1850

I affirm that Divine Mind did not 'create' the Laws of Nature; they are simply the outward manifestations of the internal essential principles which constitute Divine existence. Consequently, Divine Mind and its laws are beyond the possibility of being changed, suspended, transcended, or destroyed.

If a particular flower bud should petition for special blessings and attentions, and demand that the germ dispense the larger share of its fluids to it, the other buds may rest assured that justice will preside. So likewise, should any individual, or group of individuals, presume to demand that their deity grant them special favours, others may rest assured that Divine laws are equal and that eternal justice will preside over the distribution of life to every flower and spirit that has an existence - anywhere in the wide-spread gardens of the Divine!

When the human mind understands, in the deepest recesses of the Soul, that Divine Mind is impartial, then it will rest and be happy. An individual, thus understanding, is invincible to the invasion of false education and inherited prejudices which exist in the world. The convinced soul is not disturbed by every word of doctrine; is unmoved by the preaching of miraculous manifestations demonstrating the divine commission of any one person; is unaffected by doctrines of final judgment, eternal condemnation, or any other absurdity of the popular schools. For they know that the Divine Mind is an eternal magnet of concentrated Goodness, and that humankind's pathway is eternally onward and upward.

Oliver Lodge
Eternal Cycle of Change 1870

Consider a cloud. It manifests itself in the sky, seems to spring into existence out of the blue, and presently evaporates again and ceases to be a cloud. As invisible vapor, it continues, and as aqueous vapour it existed before it condensed into minute drops of liquid – before it took shape and form and became visible. In essence it exists all the time, and the persistent material can form another cloud or rain, or it can flow as a river, or can enter the sea, but only to evaporate again in due time, and go through an eternal cycle of change.

So it is also for an individual in an even deeper sense. That which now appears to us as sleep – sleep from which there is no waking – may really be the prelude to a state of keen activity. For sleep need not be dreamless; the spirit of an entranced person may be, and sometimes is, in an exceptional state of activity. For stillness of the body is no guarantee of stillness of the soul; nor does death of the body convey any assurance of the soul's decease.

John Caird
Infinite Inheritance 1880

Oneness of mind and will with the Divine mind and will, is not the future hope and aim of spirituality but it's very beginning and birth in the soul. To enter into the spiritual life is to terminate the struggle. In that act of self-surrender, there is identification of the finite with the eternal. Spiritual development is not progress *towards* but *within* the sphere of the infinite. It is not in the vain attempt, by endless finite increments, to become possessed of infinite wealth, but in the constant exercise of spiritual activity to claim that infinite inheritance of which we are already in possession.

Helena P. Blavatsky
Consciousness and Self-Consciousness 1888

Everything is conscious in its own way and on its own plane. But this is not to say that everything is self-conscious, or that everything has a consciousness that approximates the conditions of human consciousness. Consciousness working through a plant-form obviously results in a different condition than consciousness working through an animal-form, and this again is different than the consciousness working through human beings, and so on.

Everything in the Universe, throughout all its kingdoms, is conscious - endowed with a consciousness of its own kind and on its own plane of perception. We men must remember that just because we do not perceive any signs which we can *recognize*, we have no right to say that no consciousness exists there. There is no such thing as 'dead' or 'blind' matter, as there is no blind or unconscious Law.

Nature, taken in its abstract sense, cannot be unconscious as it is the emanation from, and thus an aspect of, the Absolute Consciousness. Who would dare to deny to vegetation, and even to minerals, a consciousness of their own? All one can say is, that this consciousness is beyond one's comprehension.

So consciousness is everywhere and in everything. The vehicles through which that consciousness works differ, and therefore the resulting display and functionality of that consciousness is different. Electricity that runs through a wire, a lightbulb, or through a computer[12]- each displays different results. The difference is not in the electricity itself, but in the material forms through which it operates.

States of Consciousness 1888

Theosophy views Nature as divided into planes of consciousness-substance. Within Nature there are distinct planes or states of substance which exist in the same 'Space', so to speak, but are not formed of the same type of substance. Therefore, these can also be viewed as distinct planes of consciousness, because beings operating therein experience each plane through a different condition of consciousness.

Whatever plane our consciousness may be acting in, both we and the things belonging to that plane are, for the time being, our only realities. As we rise in the scale of development we perceive that, during the stages through which we have passed, we mistook shadows for realities. The upward progress of the Ego is a series of progressive awakenings, each advance bringing with it the idea that now, at last, we have reached 'reality'; but only when we shall have reached the Absolute Consciousness and blended our own with it, shall we be free from the delusions produced by Maya.

---

[12] Blavatsky is likely referring to the newly invented electromagnetic keypunch machine and tabulator.

One of the most important distinctions made in theosophy in regards to how consciousness works through matter, is the distinction between what we might call regular or instinctual consciousness, and self-consciousness or reflective consciousness. Theosophy teaches that self-consciousness can only arise through a vehicle that has reached a certain degree of complexity; the nervous system needs to be complex enough to allow for self-consciousness to operate. The human brain has within it a certain degree of complexity that allows for a somewhat more complex sense of self than animals display. As the forms become more complex [from mineral, to plant, to animal, to human], consciousness is able to display itself in a more individualized manner.

William James
The Experience of Consciousness 1902

Our normal waking consciousness, rational consciousness as we call it, is but one special type of consciousness, whilst all about it, parted from it by the filmiest of screens, lie potential forms of consciousness entirely different. We may go through life without suspecting their existence; but apply the requisite stimulus and at a touch they are there in all their completeness. No account of the universe in its totality can be final which leaves these other forms of consciousness quite disregarded.

Philosophy lives in words, but truth and fact well up into our lives in ways that exceed language. There is in the living act of perception always something that glimmers and twinkles and will not be caught, and for which reflection comes too late. No one knows this as well as the philosopher. He must fire his volley of new vocables out of his conceptual shotgun, for his profession condemns him to this industry; but he secretly knows the hollowness and irrelevancy. His formulas are like photographs; they lack the depth, the motion, the vitality. In the spiritual sphere, in particular, the belief that formulas are true can never wholly take the place of personal experience.

A Believing Attitude 1896

In the trances of Leonora Piper, I cannot resist the conviction that knowledge appears which she has never gained by the ordinary waking use of her eyes and ears and wits. What the source of this knowledge may be I know not, and have not the glimmer of an explanatory suggestion to make; but from admitting the fact of such knowledge I can see no escape. So when I turn to the rest of the evidence, ghosts and all, I cannot carry with me the irreversibly negative bias of the 'rigorously scientific' mind, with its presumption as to what the true order of nature ought to be. I feel as if, though the evidence be flimsy in spots, it may nevertheless collectively carry heavy weight.

Science means, first of all, a certain dispassionate method. To suppose that it means a certain set of results that one should pin one's faith upon and hug forever is sadly to mistake its genius, and degrades the scientific body to the status of a sect. Science, when it denies such exceptional occurrences, lies prostrate in the dust for me; and the most urgent intellectual need which I feel at present is that science be built up again in a form in which such things may have a positive place.

I have brought with me tonight an essay in the justification of faith, a defence of our right to adopt a believing attitude in spiritual matters in spite of the fact that our merely logical intellect may not have been convinced. Objective evidence and certitude are doubtless very fine ideals to play with, but where on this moonlit and dream-visited planet are they found?

I live, to be sure, by the practical faith that we must go on experiencing and thinking over our experience, for only thus can our opinions grow more true; but to maintain that any one of them—I absolutely do not care which—could never be re-interpretable or corrigible, I believe to be a tremendously mistaken attitude.

There is but one certain truth—the truth that the phenomenon of consciousness exists.

Inmost Nature of Reality[13]

If we survey the field of history and ask what feature all great periods of expansion of the human mind have in common, we shall find simply this: that all of them have said to the human being, "the inmost nature of the reality is in harmony with powers which you possess." The mere assurance that my powers, such as they are, relate to that universal essence, that it speaks to them and will, in some way, recognize its reply, that I can engage within it - suffices to make it rational to my feeling.

What is Religion? 1902

Were one asked to characterize religion in the broadest and most general terms possible, one might say that it consists of the belief that there is an unseen order, and that our supreme good lies in harmoniously adjusting ourselves thereto.

Albert Einstein
Cosmic Religious Feeling 1930

There is a stage of religious experience which I shall call cosmic religious feeling. It is very difficult to elucidate this feeling to anyone who is entirely without it, especially as there is no anthropomorphic conception of God corresponding to it.

This individual feels the futility of human desires and aims and the sublimity and marvellous order which reveal themselves both in nature and in the world of thought. Individual existence impresses them as a sort of prison and they want to experience the universe as a single significant whole. Religious geniuses of all ages have been distinguished by this kind of religious feeling,

---

[13]   Published after death. Knox, Howard J. (1914). *The Philosophy of William James*. Constable and Company.

which knows no dogma and no God conceived in man's image; so that there can be no church whose central teachings are based on it. Hence it is precisely among the heretics of every age that we find those individuals who were filled with this highest kind of religious feeling.

I maintain that cosmic religious feeling is the strongest and noblest motive for scientific research. Only those who realize the immense efforts and, above all, the devotion, are able to grasp the strength of the emotion out of which such work, remote as it is from the immediate realities of life, can issue. What a deep conviction of the rationality of the universe and what a yearning to understand. It is cosmic religious feeling that gives us such strength.

Eileen Garrett
By Way of the Soul 1943

By way of the soul, the universal spirit continually animates the individual man; and by way of the soul, the individual reunites himself with the whole.

Behind the atom's dual nature, there lies that moment of creation in which the essence of the Universal becomes diffused into individualities; and eventually, the essences of those individualities are again transmuted into the undifferentiated unity of the whole. To begin to realize this process is to begin to be soul-conscious; and its psychological effect is that one begins, through understanding, to lose one's fear of both of those phases of being which we call life and death.

I do not intend this to be a religious preachment. It is sacred only in the sense that it speaks of our innate affinity with the whole, the universal Unity. It is sacred only in the sense that, in a decidedly profane and confused world, it emphasizes the free nature of the life and consciousness that are within us.

Carl G. Jung[14]
Wondrous

When one reflects upon what consciousness really is, one is profoundly impressed by the extreme wonder of the fact that an event which takes place outside in the cosmos simultaneously produces an internal image, that it takes place 'inside' as well - which is to say: it becomes conscious.

Fading Memories

Fate will have it – and this has always been the case with me - that all the outer aspects of my life were accidental. Only what is interior has proved to have substance and a determining value. As a result, all memory of outer events has faded. Perhaps these outer experiences were never so very essential anyhow, or were so only in that they coincided with phases of my inner development.

An enormous part of these outer manifestations of my life has vanished from my memory - for the very reason that I participated in them with all my energies. Yet these are the very things that make up a sensible biography: persons one has met, travels, adventures, entanglements, blows of destiny, and so on. But with few exceptions, all these things have become for me phantasms which I barely recollect, and which my mind has no desire to reconstruct, for they no longer stir my imagination.

Whence Comes Such a Dream?

I had a dream which both frightened and encouraged me. It was night in some unknown place, and I was making slow and painful headway against the mighty wind. Dense fog was everywhere. I had my hands cupped around a tiny light which threatened to go out at any moment. Everything depended upon my keeping this little light alive. Suddenly I had the feeling that

---

[14] Published after death. Jung, C. G. (1965). *Memories, Dreams, Reflections*. Vintage Books.

something was coming up behind me. I looked back and saw a gigantic black figure following me. I was conscious, in spite of my terror, that I must keep my little light going regardless of all dangers. When I awoke, I realized at once that the figure was my own shadow, brought into being by the little light I was carrying. I knew that this little light was my consciousness, the only light I have; my own understanding was the sole treasure I possessed, and the greatest.

I asked myself, "Whence comes such a dream?" Till then I had taken it for granted that such dreams were sent directly by God. But now doubts assailed me. The real question was why this process took place and why it broke through into consciousness. Consciously, I had done nothing to promote any such development; on the contrary. Something must therefore have been at work behind the scenes, some intelligence, something more intelligent than myself. For the extraordinary idea that, in the light of consciousness, the inner realm appearing as a gigantic shadow was not something I would have hit on of my own accord.

Now all at once I understood many things that had been inexplicable to me before - in particular, that cold shadow of embarrassment and estrangement which passed over people's faces whenever I alluded to anything reminiscent of the inner realm.

James Hillman
Soul & Spirit 1989

By soul I mean a perspective rather than a substance, a viewpoint toward things rather than a thing itself. This perspective is reflective; it mediates events and makes differences between ourselves and everything that happens...soul-making means differentiating this middle ground.

It is as if consciousness rests upon an inner place or deeper person or ongoing presence – that is simply there even when all our subjectivity, ego, and consciousness go into eclipse. Soul is like a reflection in a flowing mirror, or like the moon which mediates only borrowed light.

Soul refers to the deepening of events into experiences; second, the significance that soul makes possible, whether in love or in religious concern, derives from its special relation with death; and third, by soul I mean the imaginative possibility in our natures, the experiencing through reflective speculation, dream, image, and fantasy – that mode which recognizes all realities as primarily symbolic or metaphorical.

The ways of the soul and the ways of the spirit only sometimes coincide. Our distinctions are Cartesian: between outer tangible reality and inner states of mind, or between body and a fuzzy conglomerate of mind, psyche, and spirit. We have lost the third, middle position which, earlier in our tradition, was the place of soul: a world of imagination, passion, fantasy, and reflection, that is neither physical and material on the one hand, nor spiritual and abstract on the other, yet bound to them both. Soul is water to the spirit's fire. *Soul is imagination*, a cavernous treasury, whereas spirit...seeks to make all one. Look up, says spirit, gain distance; there is something beyond and above, and what is above is always, always superior.

Arthur Hastings
Resistance to Belief 2002

It seems to me that there are forces in ourselves and in society to prevent belief on certain kinds of conclusions. The resistance to belief can come from the fear of being wrong, of accepting a conclusion that will prove to be in error; asserting a belief that might be proved wrong can lead to social rejection and the risk of being humiliated; in this Western culture, the charge of being irrational is a damning one; a fear of being tarred by one's own inner critic or one's colleagues with the dirty brush of wishful thinking, enthusiasm, and emotional beliefs.

I have observed this fear-to-believe tendency in parapsychological circles. Various of my colleagues have said that we ought to accept the reality of psi [psychic phenomena] and get on to figuring out what makes it tick and how it functions for individuals and society. I think this is actually beginning to happen, but a considerable number of psi researchers still will not take a stand on the question, though the evidence is more than ample. Investigation certainly suggests other forms of consciousness, separated from our ordinary consciousness by the "filmiest of screens", as William James wrote.

With openness to whatever is given in experience, diligent reflection, and educated intuition, I believe we can identify some of the recurring elements in these non-ordinary areas of experience, accept them as established enough for belief, and then explore the consequences of that acceptance. I believe we can be open to such beliefs and still be thoughtful, be objective, have integrity, and arrive at a deeper knowledge of ourselves and reality.

Apparitions and Hallucinations 2002

Some writers and researchers have labelled out of body experiences (OBE) and near-death experiences (NDE) as hallucinations; and similarly in the psychiatric bereavement literature, the apparitions of deceased spouses are usually referred to as hallucinations.

But to call something a hallucination does not explain it. It merely offers a name that we are familiar with and causes us to lump a diversity of experiences into one dismissive category. So far as I know, there is no adequate theory of hallucinations that is grounded in brain neurology. Thus to call an apparition a hallucination, meaning that it is a fantasy, is implicitly presuming an explanation that dismisses and pathologizes it, neither of which is necessarily supported by the evidence. On the other hand, an OBE or an NDE case does not necessarily establish that the experience, such as tunnels and beings of light, are really 'over there' in another dimension. Maybe they are, and maybe not. If there is more to reality than we know, certainly our language and habitual ways of thinking are not familiar with those reaches.

Brian L. Lancaster
Quest for Transformation 2004

The quest for transformation...motivates the intense introspection associated with mystical approaches. A prerequisite of transformation is a thorough grasp of what it is that has to be transformed. Indeed, disciplined introspective knowledge is already a sign of a mind undergoing transformation. For our purposes, the key point is that the spiritual traditions contribute a first-person understanding of consciousness that is at least the equal of those available from more philosophical and scientific approaches. Any theory of consciousness that flies in the face of such understanding should be regarded as suspect.

Hartelius, Rothe & Roy
Expanding Beyond the Self 2013

Altered states of consciousness that characterize spiritual, mystical, and transcendent experience are not delusional distortions, but can be understood as perceptions and experiences associated with a self that seems expanded beyond its conventional limits.

The notion that the self is capable of expanding beyond conventional boundaries implies that self is interconnected with community and world. These experiences of expanding beyond an ordinary sense of self are sought not so much for their novelty (although this undoubtedly happens) as for their healing potential, their ability to foster an experience of meaning, purpose, and belonging in the world. A psychology of self-expansiveness is therefore engaged not only with these experiences, but with their transformative capacities.

Some scholars work to understand the world carefully and critically through the shifted lens of a transpersonal vision that understands the intimate interweaving of all life, and search for ways to extend scientific work that may be compatible with this stance - embracing scientific methods, but rejecting the often-accompanying philosophy that assumes life to be constructed of rule-following particles.[15]

Simon G. James
Mediumship and the Bereaved 2022

Modern society no longer accommodates the journey through grief in the way it once did. The gradual breakdown in religious and cultural rituals which once marked a death and allowed the bereaved to grieve safely within community – rituals such as funerals, orthodox memorials, and other shared grief scenarios - has left people spiritually and emotionally adrift. Religious institutions were once able to meet these needs by offering various formulae for the mourner which included duration of mourning, personal conduct of the bereaved, and sometimes what to expect after death. However, structured religions no longer hold sway for many today.

There is a need to construct new avenues of connection, to create modern rituals that facilitate the continuity of the post-death relationship. Some transpersonal psychotherapists aim to do this by employing a variety of effective modalities designed to integrate the grief experience and the spiritual experience.[16] That said, the focus tends to be on the inner state of the bereaved individual; in my experience, however, the bereaved are equally, if not more, concerned about the welfare of their loved one after death as with

---

[15]   Grof, S. (1983). *East and West: Ancient Wisdom and Modern Science.* Journal of Transpersonal Psychology, 15(1), 13-36.

[16]   Bella, K.A. and Serlin, I.A. (2013). *Expressive and Creative Arts Therapies.* In H. L. Friedman and G. Hartelius (Eds)., The Wiley-Blackwell Handbook of Transpersonal Psychology (pp. 529-543). Wiley-Blackwell.

their own pain, and many find comfort in coming together with someone who has some understanding of the afterlife experience.

The very fact that someone has chosen to see a medium suggests that they already have some notion of 'other'. Both medium and sitter tacitly agreeing to co-create a new paradigm of belief. In doing so, they embark on a mythic journey of transformation, moving into "the natural and indispensable intermediate stage between unconscious and conscious cognition."[17] The act of sitting with a medium then becomes a vehicle for psychospiritual movement.[18] By removing the obstacles to reunification through communication with the other world, one minimizes the more debilitating effects of grief. This then creates a clearer pathway for the forward movement of the individual from a place of pain to a place of relative acceptance.

Brian S. Robertson
Being Spiritual, Being Human 2022

The medium's spiritual, mental, emotional and physical health are the foundation of healthy mediumship. Discovering our true nature, unfolding all of our talents, and being fully in the world, are essential to doing good work as a medium. A medium must also develop their sensitivity to a heightened degree, but this is often the very quality that makes us vulnerable to personal distress, instability, and lack of confidence, especially when working alone without community support.

These imbalances, when taken to extremes, potentially constitute the shadow side of mediumistic sensitivity. Unfortunately, this is a subject not often addressed in the world of mediumship where being 'spiritual' generally equates with radiating love and light to the exclusion of other less savoury emotions.

---

[17] Jung, C. G. (1965). *Memories, Dreams, Reflections*. Vintage Books.

[18] Osborne, G., & Bacon, A. (2015). *The Working Life of a Medium: A Qualitative Examination of Mediumship as a Support Service for the Bereaved*. Mental Health, Religion & Culture.

I believe that, in order to be fully spiritual, one must be fully human. This involves what Jung called assimilation of the shadow. Only then may we begin to see the emergence of the whole medium and therefore offer our best service to those in need. It is important that spirituality "not be presented in an idealized form in which its shadow is ignored. Its capacity to be terrifyingly awful as well as inspiringly awesome must be recognized, as spirituality is no mere bromide, but the deepest and most profound issue that can be imagined."[19]

[19] Hartelius, G., Rothe, G., & Roy, P. (2013). *Brand for the Burning*. In H. L. Friedman & G. Hartelius (Eds.), The Wiley-Blackwell Handbook of Transpersonal Psychology, Wiley Blackwell.

CHAPTER FOUR

Spiritual Development

Andrew Jackson Davis
True Education 1893

> *A pebble in the streamlet scant*
> *Has changed the course of many a river,*
> *A dew-drop on the baby plant*
> *Has warped the giant oak forever.*

A child is the repository of infinite possibilities. Enfolded in the human infant is the beautiful image of an imperishable and perfect being. The Divine image is within. It is the goal of true education to develop that image, and in such a way that individuality shall not be impaired, but rather revealed in its own fullness and personal perfection. The highest aim of education is to reveal the life and the form of that individual perfection which Divine Wisdom has implanted in the human spirit.

Charles Wentworth Upham
Beauty 1857

I have come to the conclusion that if men and women wish to realize the full power of personal beauty, it must be by cherishing noble hopes and purposes, by having something to do and something to live for. By expanding the soul, it gives expansion and symmetry to the very body which contains it.

Anonymous
How the Thing is to be Done 1857

Our experiences must be entirely our own. To sit in a public place and listen to another's experience, is not to get an experience that is calculated to do us any good. When we move, we must go alone.

It has been said that we hunt far and wide for truth when it is right in the road before us. We look through telescopes when we would be better accepting such facts as lie directly in our way. Man's reformation is to come about by his own resolute endeavour. No one else can do it for him. The world will not be renovated until every living person in it begins to reform himself. Upon individual effort and individual aspiration all depends. We must change ourselves before we can hope to work any influence upon others. Others must be able to behold beauty in us and then perhaps they will be attracted by the example.

We have to fall back upon ourselves and trust to the power and spirit of the individual. Reforms properly begin at home. They must work in the heart of the reformer first. And until this truth is better understood, and more generally practised upon, we shall hope in vain for any change that will be either thorough or abiding.

Alexander Calder
Sitting in Silence 1878

Meditation is a powerful aid to spiritual growth. If we stand apart each day from the noise and tumult around, we commune with ourselves and come more in contact with the unseen. We experience, by this very abstraction and silence, a deepening effect on the soul and an opportunity for fixing our hearts on important truths. The seed of life needs to sink deep into the soil of our minds before it can take root, so as to bring forth something more than leaves. Knowledge of the right sort must also be grounded into a firm base.

I refer not to such meditation as leads to senseless reverie and asceticism, but to that established on intelligence which arouses the spirit to activity, quickening it into life. For in the conscience lies the light to guide and shape our conduct, truth being the oil with which it should be fed. If we would but follow that light with sincerity, it would educate, protect, and lead into the way of safety. It imparts a satisfaction with which nothing can compare, for it carries us beyond this life. And this light burns brighter and more powerfully the more it is used. It increases in strength, endowing us with the requisite power to carry us through the world by illuminating our whole existence.

Let us set our minds and hearts diligently to the cultivation of qualities which brighten our spiritual health - kindness, humility, moderation, industry, and love. Active daily introspection, a careful questioning of the soul, an unflinching scrutiny into its thoughts, words, purposes, and acts - by this process, the spirit obtains the true dignity of spiritual life. This, I humbly think, is the phenomenon we should prize and study to promote, for it concerns the construction of character and the wealth of our souls.

The sooner religion is freed from all the mystery of creeds, fashion, and forms, and the simple components of moral and spiritual culture directly applied to daily life, the better will be the condition of mankind; for we will then become the possessors of a process of self-government, and not be subject to feeble opinions and equally frail fancies.

Thomas Burnside
Active Cultivation 1880

There is an erroneous idea that if a medium waits patiently and thinks of nothing, they will receive a perfect shower of spiritual blessings, and be transformed at once into an intellectual prodigy.

What would we think if someone, ignorant of music, said they intended to sit in a circle until it all came to them, and that they expected their compositions would excel those of Handel or Mozart? It is action, and not a listless apathy born of careless expectancy, which ensures success. The farmer endeavours to enrich the soil so that the seed may bear fruit; and so the enquirer should enrich the mind by every means in their power, so that the thoughts from the spirit world may be the more easily impressed upon them and find suitable expression.

Of course, care must be taken that the mind remains free from prejudice and bigotry, as they steel the mind against spirit impressions. Excess of learning is of little use if it is nurtured in prejudice, as one then becomes ignorant through learning.

Whilst pains should be taken to cultivate the mind, a portion of time should be devoted each day to waiting in the quiet, and by degrees the mind will become accustomed to withdraw itself from the contemplation of mundane affairs. But action is the great staple upon which everything progressive is hinged. So let us be active, mentally and physically, and we will reap our just reward. Let us bring about success by exercising our brains to store the mind with useful knowledge, and so build up a glorious superstructure for the indwelling of the eternal spirit.

Helen Temple Brigham
Seek for Yourself 1920

Divine truth was not compressed into one book, given to one leader, or to one helper of humanity. It was given as a truth to all the ages. It is for humankind to seek for it, to understand it, and to apply it.

You must think for yourself and so learn the truth. Think earnestly, reasonably and rationally. Consider, weigh, measure, sift, analyse, and you will find in those things which the world declares valueless, golden grains of truth. You will sift that which comes to you and the chaff will blow away; the residue will be that which is most valuable, having within itself the answer to your question. There is proof on every side. Seek for yourself.

Ernest S. Holmes
Wholeness 1934

The advancement of science, philosophy and religion is not the result of a change in the nature of Reality, but a change in our minds toward Reality.

If we have made discoveries of physical and material laws, should it seem strange that we might also make discoveries of mental and spiritual laws? Indeed, the great discoveries of the future will be in these very realms. Science, philosophy, intuition, and revelation must unite in an impersonal effort if Truth is to be gained and held. No system of thought can endure which denies human experiences; no religion can be vital which separates humanity from divinity.

Human beings are more than matter. There is an inner life higher than the psyche. A human being is mind, soul and body; mental, spiritual and physical; intelligence, volition and will, fused into a coordinated personality, and one can understand oneself only from the larger viewpoint. We deal with the real person only when we deal with the whole person. We deal with the whole person only when we deal with mental, physical and spiritual faculties working in unity.

Eileen Garrett
The Golden Key 1943

There is an ancient legend which tells that at a council of the gods, they were considering where they should hide the golden key to man's destiny, so that he should not find it too easily (and so become god-like). They hit up on the clever idea of hiding it where man would be least likely to look for it – deep within himself. And there it has remained hidden throughout the ages.

Disappointed in our long search within the objective realms of existence, and distressed by the repeated failure of our own creations to fulfil the needs of our lives, we are turning back upon ourselves and catching glimpses of our own inner nature. We have caught an intuitive flash of insight, revealing the way. And though we are slow to turn from all the marvellous achievements of the past, we can never escape from the effects of that mystical moment of psychic perception.

Actually, we do not have to turn away from anything real. We are rooted in the physical world, and could not abandon it if we would. What we have to turn away from is our illusion of the importance of parts. We must focus awareness in an ever-evolving perception of the whole, and progressively set our natures free through the outward play of experience, sympathy, and understanding. The pioneers in life have left us maps and memoranda (symbols) which, if we will use them, will lead us smoothly to a new psychological peak.

Carl G. Jung
Developing the Whole Person[20]

I have frequently seen people become neurotic when they content themselves with inadequate answers to the questions of life. They seek position, marriage, reputation, upward success or money, and remain unhappy and neurotic even when they have attained what they were seeking. Such people are usually confined within too narrow a spiritual horizon. Theirs has not sufficient content, sufficient meaning. If they are enabled to develop into more spacious personalities, the neurosis generally disappears. For

---

[20] Published after death. Jung, C. G. (1965). *Memories, Dreams, Reflections.* Vintage Books

that reason, the idea of development was always of the highest importance to me.

Frederic W. H. Meyers
Prayer[21]

I am glad that you've asked me about prayer because I have rather strong ideas on the subject.

There exists around us a spiritual universe, and that universe is in actual relation with the material. From the spiritual universe comes the energy which maintains the material; the energy which makes the life of each individual spirit. Our spirits are supported by a perpetual indrawl of this energy, and the vigour of that indrawl is perpetually changing. Plainly, we must endeavour to draw in as much spiritual life as possible and place our minds in any attitude favourable to such indrawl. *Prayer* is the general name for that attitude of open and earnest expectancy.

If we then ask to *whom* to pray, the answer (strangely enough) must be that that does not much matter. Prayer is an increase in intensity of absorption of spiritual power or grace; but we do not know enough of what takes place in the spiritual world to know how the prayer operates, *who* is cognizant of it, or through what channel the grace is given.

Ena Twigg
The Need to Know 1973

Youth wants to know. I believe they are trying to find something of value. They are searching for a higher level of consciousness. And now, many are turning to a spirituality without labels, for the young don't want or need them.

I would like to say to the young people who are looking for answers, but sometimes don't know how to ask the question – start

---

[21]   Found in: James, William. (1902). *The Varieties of Religious Experience.* Longmans, Green & Co..

with, "Who am I? What am I?" Meditate and think. Find places where you can pursue your research. Form communities or join groups where these things can be discussed and debated. Study the works of great minds who have investigated the subject.

The thing that we should be striving to teach young people is how to think positively and constructively, how to think on all the beauty of the world. For we co-create the universe with the Divine.

Coral Polge
A Silent Truth 1991

"Have I travelled very far on the road between illusion and truth?" I ask myself, often thinking of the words spoken by my husband when discussing my mystical experiences with him. "You have found truth," he had said. "Now you must work to *become* it."

We all find truth in our individual ways eventually. Some seekers use meditation to know themselves, and thereby find the creative life force, the over-self, the cosmic consciousness - call it what you will; but labels simply cause antagonism. Words create divisions, for truth is a silent knowing; and all dogmas, 'isms', and beliefs that 'our way' makes us specially chosen people, only drive us further from spiritual oneness.

Some people, like me, simply find truth through the buffeting which life gives us all. But what a long, long road there is ahead before I become one with that truth, a road which, for me, must be service through my portraits. If I live to be ninety, I will never be happy with the quality of the work, certainly from an artistic point of view. But if only one in a hundred of my clients receives some evidence which helps them to know that love is an eternal bond, then I shall feel it has been worthwhile. As long as there is somebody's picture waiting to be drawn, I will continue to be used as a channel for such communication between this world and the next. This was the path mapped out for me. It is a path I tread with love and a great sense of privilege that I was chosen to do so.

Ray Woollam
Fictitious Hindsight 1989

It seems to me that our most preposterous cultural superstition is the belief in the existence of a duality called 'good' and 'bad'. This superstition can be so all-consuming that the human mind is sometimes full of little else. Furthermore, the assumptions that good-bad, right-wrong, and should-should not have actual substance are often so completely accepted that they are never questioned.

When value judgements are applied to the past, memory becomes partially or entirely obliterated. It rusts shut. I often notice that the person who value-judges has little or no ability to remember in a natural way. They are seldom able to recall a moment in time and to re-experience it as though they were there once again, looking out with their own eyes, and feeling or thinking as they once did. Instead, imagination takes over and they 'bin' their earlier experiences as either 'good' or 'bad'. In so doing, imagination may completely displace memory. There are a few ways I notice this.

Firstly, an actual memory does not result in seeing myself objectively; but rather, I look *out* of my eyes and see only what I saw then. Secondly, an actual memory will usually involve a moving, changing scene; still-life snapshots indicate distortions of reality, creations of the imagination. Thirdly, if there is a 'good-bad' caption or story attached, I am probably producing another fictitious chapter in the novel of my life. I can be sure that when I recall my 'good-bad' decisions, I'm caught up in the process of fictitious hindsight.

In real life, there is no possibility of making good choices or bad choices, for every choice is made at a point in time and every decision, when it was made, was made for a reason. When I'm *actually* remembering any decision that I ever made, I will clearly remember how I saw it - then, and what were my reasons - then. To whit, there are no mistakes!

James Hillman
The Real Heart 1989

One day in Burgholzli, the famous institute in Zürich where the words *schizophrenia* and *complex* were born, I watched a woman being interviewed. She sat in a wheelchair because she was elderly and feeble. She said that she was dead, for she lost her heart. The psychiatrist asked her to place her hand over her breast and feel her heart beating: it must still be there if she could feel its beat. "That," she said, "is not my real heart." She and the psychiatrist looked at each other. There was nothing more to say. She had lost the loving courageous connection to life – and that is the real heart, not the ticker which can as well pulsate isolated in a glass bottle.

Michael Daniels
Transport or Transform? 2005

A psychic or other paranormal experience is not necessarily transformational. If a transpersonal[22] experience has no transformational effect, then it has simply been an entertaining diversion. This is true, I believe, no matter how extraordinary, ecstatic, delightful, or profound the experience may seem to be.

To draw a parallel with a dramatic performance...Schechner[23] suggests that theatre may induce either temporary transportations of consciousness in performers and audience, or permanent

---

[22]   "Transpersonal psychology is a transformative psychology of the whole person in intimate relationship with an interconnected and evolving world; it pays special attention to self-expansive states as well as to spiritual, mystical, and other exceptional human experiences that gain meaning in such a context" (Hartelius, Rothe, & Roy, 2013).

[23]   Schechner, R. (1988). *Performance Theory*. New York: Routledge.

transformations. In exactly the same way, I believe, paranormal experiences (or other altered states) may be either *transportative* or *transformative*. Only if they are truly transformational should they be considered genuinely transpersonal. From the perspective of parapsychology, on the other hand, paranormal experiences are of interest only to the extent that they are able to demonstrate objectively the *reality* of paranormal phenomena.

This discussion helps also to place into context the warnings that are often given about the spiritual dangers of dabbling with the paranormal. In my view these very real dangers result when a paranormal experience produces a retreat into superstitious and magical thinking, or even into psychosis.[24] As a direct consequence, the person may then become open to abuse and exploitation by unscrupulous people who are capable of manipulating this vulnerable position.

There is also a danger that the ordinary world of personal and social experience may be considered relatively unimportant. It is therefore important always to bring the transpersonal into our everyday lives and, in this way, to 'ground' our mystical experience; to encourage people to face up to their paranormal experiences, to find a way of integrating them meaningfully into their life and, ultimately, to allow them to lead towards development beyond the self.

Robin Wall Kimmerer
Gifts 2013

Many indigenous peoples share the understanding that we are each endowed with a particular gift, a unique ability. Birds to sing and stars to glitter, for instance. It is understood that these gifts have a dual nature, though: a gift is also a responsibility. If the bird's gift is song, then it has a responsibility to greet the day with music. It is the duty of birds to sing and the rest of us receive the

---

[24] Grof, S. (2000). *Psychology of the Future: Lessons from Modern Consciousness Research.* State University of New York Press.

song as a gift. Asking what is our responsibility is perhaps also to ask, What is our gift? And how shall we use it?

Brian S. Robertson & Simon G. James
Spiritual Movement 2017

Those of us who seek a spiritual life, who wish to touch the divine heartbeat of creation, must allow movement. Movement is change. Sometimes we only move when things are no longer comfortable for us.

Those of us who seek a spiritual life do so because we are no longer content with what was. We must move. In doing so, we choose to embrace the changes that bring us back to our true nature. The conscious intention to unfold our true nature and thereby reveal more of the Divine within us is a choice of the mind, prompted by the movement of the soul, to fulfil the destiny of the spirit.

Everything We Think and Do 2017

There are no special divine dispensations and no miracles. There is simply the immutable, beautiful and eternal natural law of cause and effect.

The choices we make have resonances as we move through life to death, and to life again. As Pythagoras said, "There is no word or action but has its echo in Eternity. Thought is an Idea in transit which, when once released, can never be lured back...all that thou thinkest, sayest, or doest bears perpetual record of itself, enduring for Eternity."

When we awaken to the power of this principle, when we understand that what we think, say and do always creates a balancing outcome, we become free.

With freedom comes responsibility for our own actions, in the realization that we ourselves have the means to effect inner change, thereby affecting the outer world.

Terry Patten
Spiritual Bypassing 2018

There is an alarming tendency in spiritual circles to resort to easy answers to hard questions, to dwell in superficial compassion, cheerfulness, and premature forgiveness, but with no willingness to understand or confront our ecological emergency, or the dire structural injustice that supports it. Thousands of well-meaning people have gone unconscious, entrained into habits they imagine are 'spiritual' but that actually reinforce irresponsible bypassing and dissociation.

Spiritual life involves growing into a wise and healthy relationship to reality. The word 'spiritual' points to the deepest level of being—essential and existential. Spiritual growth and development enable us to glimpse the bountiful grace in which we live—the beauty of the world, and the privilege of conscious embodied existence. Gratitude is universal spiritual wisdom, and it is sufficient. Such gratitude is awake. It is realistically in touch with loss and death and threat—not in denial.

CHAPTER FIVE

A Social Conscience

Andrew Jackson Davis
Individual Freedom 1860

No one need fear the sovereignty of individualism – that is, the right of each to act in accordance with his highest intuitions. For, should one person overstep their boundaries, another will let them know it. However, we need to practice the gospel of self-government. The conservative may cry aloud for the safety and sanctity of institutions. But heed them not! Their cries proceed from the marshes of dictatorship which are ten-fold more dangerous than the everglades of Florida.

John Page Hopps
An Agonised Appeal 1870

Mrs. Y, a lady by birth, education, and intelligence, is incarcerated in the most horrible of confinements, a lunatic asylum, for being conscientiously compelled to admit that she believes in an existence after death and the possibility of communion with those who have passed. Agonized appeals for her release are met by the scornful incredulity of the *Commissioners in Lunacy*, assured that anyone holding such a doctrine cannot be in their right reason.

At last, on being released from prison, she writes to Lord Cairns requesting a public inquiry into the circumstances of her detention; the Lord Chancellor informed her that "he has no power to interfere in the matter." Mrs. Y then addressed herself to Lord Shaftsbury, as the chairman of the *Lunacy Commissioners,* and now added a number of other charges, many of them being for the grossest and most indefensible offenses. Her indictment is, however, politely waived.

And here for the present, the matter ends, but where it may reopen, and whom the abyss of shame and sorrow may next engulf, it is impossible to predict. It only remains for those with similar beliefs to be on their guard.

A God that None Can See 1873

The abuses of lunatic asylums are becoming alarmingly too common. We have, of late, had disgusting revelations of the cruelties practised upon patients. Mrs. X appears to be as sane as any of her captors or judges. This victim of neglect and cruelty is an intelligent, well-educated, and particularly sane woman who believes what hundreds of thousands of the brightest people in the world now believe – that, in certain circumstances and under certain conditions, the spirit world can make their presence known and give indications of their wishes. The fools who dealt with her did not manage to drive her mad as they might have done, and she lives to tell the story.

In reply to a question as to whether she could appeal to a jury, one of the *Commissioners in Lunacy* answered, "It is very possible, but very undesirable; we always advise ladies under these circumstances to keep quiet." When she stood before Justice Blackburn, the judge said that belief in the moving hand by a spiritual being looked like insanity. So it does. In reply, counsel on behalf of the lady in question very shrewdly said, that if any of the theological beliefs so dear to most people were taken out of context, they too would appear grotesque and insane to the onlooker. Take the act of prayer. How would it look to one who had never taken part in prayer to see people shut their eyes and talk to someone who nobody could see? You say that it is an insanity to believe the spirit can control the hand of one person, and yet you say that it is perfectly reasonable to believe that a spirit (God) can direct the destinies of every creature in the world.

People who talk about mediumship in connection with insanity must be recklessly determined to push ignorant prejudice to the verge of criminal prosecution.

J. Frank Baxter
What We Stand For 1891

The all of Spiritualism is not spirit communication or manifestation. Spiritualism has a deeper and grander meaning – the renovation of church, society, and state, and practical work against all things which fetter the mind. It teaches that, better than being a Jew, a Catholic, a priest, or a Spiritualist, is *being a true man or woman*; and so too in the political arena - better than being a Democrat, a Republican, or one of any party, is being a true man or woman in whatever position one feels to take.

Had not this latest revival, called Modern Spiritualism, come to be, human slavery might still be in existence in our country. Spiritualism as a religion has nothing more to do with the state than should the church have, and that is *nothing at all*; but it is a natural development as a matter of phenomena and as a science. Remember, Spiritualism is not man-made - theologies are.

Albert Einstein
Community 1934

When we survey our lives and endeavours, we soon observe that almost the whole of our actions and desires is bound up with the existence of other human beings. We have, therefore, to admit that we owe our principal advantage to the fact of living in human society. The individual is what he is and has the significance that he has, not so much in virtue of his individuality, but rather as a member of a great human community which directs his material and spiritual existence from the cradle to the grave. A man's value to the community depends primarily on how far his feelings, thoughts, and actions are directed toward promoting the good of his fellows.

All the valuable achievements, material, spiritual, and moral, which we receive from society have been brought about in the course of countless generations by creative individuals. Someone once discovered the use of fire, someone the cultivation of edible plants, and someone the steam engine. Without creative personalities able to think and judge independently, the upward development of society is as unthinkable as the development of the individual personality without the nourishing soil of the community.

A Kind of Freedom 1940

The development of science and of the creative activities of the spirit in general require still another kind of freedom, which may be characterized as inward freedom.

It is this freedom of the spirit which consists in the independence of thought from the restrictions of authoritarian and social prejudices as well as from habit in general. This inward freedom is an infrequent gift of nature and a worthy objective for the individual. Yet the community can do much to further this by not interfering with its development. Only if outward and inner freedom are constantly and consciously pursued is there a possibility of spiritual development and, thus, of improving man's outward and inner life.

Not Written in the Stars 1954

In talking about human rights today, we are referring primarily to the following demands: protection of the individual against arbitrary infringement by other individuals or by the government;

the right to work and adequate earnings from that work; freedom of discussion and teaching; participation of the individual in the formation of his government. These human rights are nowadays recognized theoretically although, by abundant use of formalistic, legal manoeuvres, they are being violated to a much greater extent than even a generation ago. The existence and validity of human rights are not written in the stars.

The ideals concerning the conduct of men toward each other and the desirable structure of the community have been conceived and taught by enlightened individuals in the course of history. Those ideals and convictions which resulted from historical experience, from the craving for beauty and harmony, have been readily accepted in theory by man - and at all times have been trampled upon by the same people under the pressure of their animal instincts. A large part of history is therefore replete with the struggle for those human rights, an eternal struggle in which a final victory can never be won. But to tire in that struggle would mean the ruin of society.

Nationalism & War 1948

We scientists, whose tragic destination has been to help in making the methods of annihilation more gruesome and more effective, must consider it our solemn and transcendent duty to do all in our power in preventing these weapons from being used for the brutal purpose for which they were invented. What task could possibly be more important for us? What social aim could be closer to our hearts?

We must build spiritual and scientific bridges linking the nations of the world. We must overcome the horrible obstacles of national frontiers. Will the peoples of the world have enough courage to overcome their own national ties to the extent that is necessary to induce them to change their deep-rooted national traditions in a most radical fashion? A tremendous effort is indispensable.

Ena Twigg
Unity of Humankind 1973

If people would stop and catch their breath, and just think of something other than themselves; if they could, for a moment, think and feel that they were one with every other person, plant, animal, and star in the sky, then we could banish wars, prejudice, and poverty. That is what we [mediums] are here for.

I see the turmoil in which we are living as man's efforts to cleanse himself and find something of value. He doesn't want a label - Muslim, Hindu, Christian, Jewish, black, white, yellow, or brown. He wants to say, "I am a human being – and I am part of the Divine." People need to free themselves from the bonds they have created for themselves. Out of all this turmoil will come our new age. I believe it has already begun.

Let us hope that the abolition of the existing international anarchy will not need to be bought by a self-inflicted world catastrophe the dimensions of which none of us can possibly imagine. The time is terribly short. We must act now if we are to act at all.

Ray Woollam
Individual Responsibility 1989

We have been given glimpses of environmental changes that are occurring more rapidly than had been previously anticipated. Will our leaders and experts in science, business, national defence, and government determine whether our children survive on a lovely planet as delightful as the one that you and I have known? Or will our planet survive at all?

These choices are made daily by each individual. Furthermore, we live in a time and place when our leaders follow *us*. The world of human affairs is determined by individuals. Individually we have the ability to think and choose. It is as individuals that we choose either the path of sanity and change, or the path of daydream and thoughtlessness.

James Hillman
The Desert 1989

The question of evil refers primarily to the anesthetised heart, the heart that has no reaction to what it faces, thereby turning the variegated sensuous face of the world into monotony, sameness, oneness. The desert of modernity. Surprisingly, this desert is not heartless, because the desert is where the lion lives…if we wish to find a responsive heart again, we must go where it seems to be least present.

According to *Physiologus* (the traditional lore of animal psychology), the lion's cubs are stillborn. They must be awakened into life by a roar. That is why the lion has such a roar: to awaken the young lions asleep, as they sleep in our hearts. What is passive, immobile, asleep in the heart creates a desert which can only be cured by its own parenting principle that shows its awakening care by roaring. The more our desert, the more we must rage, which rage is love.

The desert is not in Egypt; it is anywhere once we desert the heart. Our way through the desert of life, or any moment in life is the awakening to it as a desert, the awakening of the beast, that vigil of desire, it's greedy paw, hot and sleepless as the sun, fulminating as sulfur, setting the soul on fire. Like cures like: the desert beast is our guardian in the desert of modern bureaucracy, ugly urbanism, academic trivialities, professional official soullessness, the desert of our ignoble condition.

We fear that rage. We dare not roar. With Auschwitz behind us, and the bomb over the horizon, we let the little lions sleep in front of the television. The heart now becomes a beast in a lair readying its attack.

Brian L. Lancaster
Overcoming the Self 2004

Ideas accepted within one long-standing tradition may be incompatible with those central to another. Indeed, the grim history of inter-religious conflicts seems to mitigate against [weaken] the validity of the kinds of truth claims often found at the heart of the conflicts. Moreover, the birth of one religion from a 'parent' is generally attributable to the 'daughter' religion advocating a position at odds with the parent, as in the case of Buddhism's development from Hinduism, for example.

Although there are many significant details in the testimonies of mystics which are indeed difficult to reconcile with each other, there is sufficient of a common core to uphold their value for our study of consciousness. For Ferrer,[25] the common core concerns... *"the overcoming of self-centeredness,* and thus a liberation from corresponding limiting perspectives and understandings."

Spiritual and mystical teachings can reveal to us the ways in which self intrudes as a limiting factor in consciousness, together with insights into the form consciousness takes when such limitation is transcended. A slightly differently nuanced emphasis is given by Dupré[26] when he suggests that the common feature in mystical testimonies involves a seeming shift in the centre of awareness from the self to 'a point beyond the self'. I am suggesting that such testimonies can be valuable in thinking about the nature of such a region beyond the self.

Robin Wall Kimmerer
From Despair to Action 2013

Until we can grieve for our planet we cannot love it. Grieving is a sign of spiritual health. But it is not enough to weep for our lost landscapes; we have to put our hands in the earth to make ourselves whole again.

---

25   Ferrer. J. N. (2002). *Revisioning Transpersonal Theory: A Participatory Vision of Human Spirituality.* State University of New York Press.

26   Dupré, L. (1989). *Unio Mystica: The State and the Experience.* In M. Idel & B. McGinn (eds.), found in "Mystical Union and Monotheistic Faith: An Ecumenical Dialogue". Macmillan.

We are deluged by information regarding our destruction of the world and hear almost nothing about how to nurture it. It is no surprise then that environmentalism becomes synonymous with dire predictions and powerless feelings. Our natural inclination to do right by the world is stifled, breeding despair when it should be inspiring action....

Despair is paralysis. It robs us of agency. It blinds us to our own power and the power of the earth. Environmental despair is a poison every bit as destructive as the methylated mercury in the bottom of Onondaga Lake. But how can we submit to despair while the land is saying, "Help"? Restoration is a powerful antidote to despair. Restoration offers concrete means by which humans can once again enter into positive, creative relationship with the more-than-human world, meeting responsibilities that are simultaneously material and spiritual.

It's not enough to grieve. It's not enough to just stop doing bad things. We have enjoyed the feast generously laid out for us by Mother Earth, but now the plates are empty and the dining room is a mess. It's time we started doing the dishes in Mother Earth's kitchen. Doing dishes has gotten a bad rap, but everyone who migrates to the kitchen after a meal knows that that's where the laughter happens, the good conversations, the friendships. Doing dishes, like doing restoration, forms relationships.

Terry Patten
Spiritual Activism 2018

Everything we love is mortal, even the living Earth. Everything regenerates, and yet is also wounded and under threat. The heart breaks to see the destruction of vulnerable people, living creatures, and wild places. We want to protect them. We want to help. As Joanna Macy so sagely puts it, "If everyone I love is in danger, I want to be here, so I can do what I can." Activism is simply acting on the impulse to "be of benefit" to something greater than yourself, in a whole variety of ways. Not all of them look like overt 'activism', but many do. All are natural expressions of human maturity. But exactly how can we effectively address the totality of this crisis?

It will ultimately require revolutionary changes in human consciousness, behaviour, culture, and the physical, economic, and political infrastructure of our whole civilization. It is so vast and intricate, it easily seems impossible. We might be tempted to despair, but despair easily becomes a self-fulfilling prophecy. And yet, because this huge transformation has so many aspects, every one of us can readily find ways to magnify love and sanity and beauty and truth and human connection. Every one of us can find many things we can actually do.

The first stage of the journey into spiritual activism is grounded robustly in gratitude and appreciation. In the second stage, we awaken from denial, apprehend the enormity of the challenge before us, and allow a great grieving process to transform the soul. We benefit even from the awful moments of hopelessness— because despair is not just the end of our conventional hope. It is also the beginning point for a new possibility.

Mature, responsible adults are charged with staying intelligently related to the realities of our lives. But that requires us to pass through all the harrowing stages of grief into acceptance. True acceptance recognizes the reality of our situation and accepts responsibility. We choose engagement with reality, including the gritty and not always pleasant involvements with people we may not like and situations we would prefer to avoid. We know we have arrived in acceptance when we are in motion, doing what we can to make a positive difference.

Brian S. Robertson
A Community for Mediums 2022

The dissociative faculty inherent in the practice of mediumship[27] is intrinsically taxing to the mind and, left unmonitored, can result in a crisis of development. The personal risks for an isolated mediumistic practitioner may include pathologically dissociative symptoms, isolation and, in my experience, a diminished mediumistic faculty over time. Such lack of individual monitoring and supervision also raises a considerable concern for the welfare of those vulnerable recipients who engage their services.

During the late 19th and early 20th centuries, the need for peer support during mediumistic development was partly met by the home circle, wherein small groups gathered privately "to identify and develop mediumistic abilities among a selected group of people often linked by kinship or friendship."[28] They provided opportunities for younger mediums to unfold their faculty within a supportive community, in an oral tradition of one-on-one training from experienced mediums.

However, the gradual decline of spiritual communities during the 21st century has since left developing mediums to fend for themselves; it has left a void in the mentorship and growth of mediums and, subsequently, an absence of those important psychological checks and balances once provided by peers in community.

Some physical 'communities' today host demonstrations of psychism and mediumship, offer private readings and sittings, and are a popular seasonal gathering place for those wishing to witness phenomena or receive messages from their loved ones. However,

---

27 Peres, J., Moreira-Almeida, A., Caixeta, L., Leao, F., & Newberg, A. (2012). *Neuroimaging During Trance State: A Contribution to the Study of Dissociation.* PloS One, 7(11).

28 McMullin, S. (2004) *Anatomy of a Séance.* McGill-Queens' University Press.

the healthy holistic development of the mediums themselves is not generally within their purview.

By 'community', I mean "groups that inspire their members in ways that promote a sense of self-discovery and group connection, encourage members to express their beliefs and values, and build relationships with others."[29] Community among mediums offering continued support, guidance, and direction is absolutely essential to their healthy and ethical development in wholeness.

---

[29] Celestine, N. (2016). *10 traits that make a positive community.* In Alice Mah & Mick Carpenter (Eds.), "Community", Blackwell Encyclopedia of Sociology. John Wiley & Sons, Ltd.

CHAPTER SIX

Glimpses of a Time

Anecdotes, Letters to the Editor, Social Events, Advertisements, and Other Curious Contributions to the Periodicals of the Era.

Light Relief

―――――⊳―0―⊲―――――

Clergyman Expelled
1857

The Wesleyan Methodist Conference, now in session at Toronto, has expelled two of its ministers - the Reverend Mr. Haugh for carrying a pistol to shoot a young man who had eloped with his daughter, and the Reverend Mr. Jones because he jilted a young lady for a better match.

Black Country Superstition
1874

In the *Dudley Herald* of last week appeared this account:

> Not one hundred miles from here, some twelve months ago, a young man died suddenly. A few weeks after his funeral, his mother was observed by a neighbour hanging out a line-full of apparel such as stockings, shirts, waistcoats, and trousers,

neckties, nightcaps, & so on. Somewhat surprised, she asked the woman why she had washed such a strange medley of articles.

"Because," replied the woman, "our Sam couldn't rest in his grave."

"Not rest in his grave?" questioned the neighbour with still greater surprise. "How do you know that?"

"Why, because," answered the woman, "since his funeral he's been seen a time or two, and I've been told if I was to wash up all his things he'd be able to rest peacefully in his grave."

The question remains how far the spirit could be affected by the washing of the clothes.— *Editor.*

Fashionable Grief for the Departed
Baroness Adelma Vay

Dear Sarah, darling John is dead!
My heart is very sore:
I have the sweetest mourning suit
Just come from Shoolbred's store.

Ah, well! our loss is but his gain,
Insurance covers all,
No more I hear his cheerful voice,
His footsteps in the hall.

My dress is trimmed with real lace,
We had four doctors here;
They call it "softening of the brain",
My bonnet is a dear!

I know your sympathy is mine;
My heartstrings almost broke;
"Dear wife, my fortune will be yours!"
Were the last words he spoke.

I've kept a lock of precious hair,
His bank-books and his will,
By which he left me all his wealth
In railroad, bank, and mill.

There's balm in Gilead I know,
And I may find relief:
Please send the latest fashions to:
Your friend in deepest grief.

Sad to See You Go
1891

Reverend Heber Newton's accuser, the Anglican monk Ignatius, is reportedly about to return to Llanthony Abbey in Great Britain where he can figure out at his leisure, says a Yankee daily, "the amount of good he has done by coming over here and interfering in other people's business."

Ghosts
1923

While most people are afraid of ghosts, even when they don't believe in them, a few prosaic people have a matter-of-fact way of dealing with visitors from 'beyond the bourn'. There is a story of a cold-blooded commercial traveller who, while sleeping at an inn, was awakened by a ghost who complained that he had been murdered in the room a century or so before. The traveller expressed his regrets with a yawn. "But," said he, "it's no business of mine. You must apply to the proper authorities. Good night!"

At Odds

We hear—'twas once a frequent boast—
   The Scientist rejects the Ghost;
But it may be, the Ghost exists
And disbelieves in Scientists!

Varieties of Intoxication
1923

A man who had seen a ghost reported the matter to a cynical friend, and was told that he was evidently not a strict teetotaller. So he challenged the unbeliever to go to the scene of the haunting and see for himself. The sceptic complied but returned saying that, for his part, he had seen nothing. "Then," said his friend, "I maintain that, just as there is a stage of intoxication in which a man may see things that are not there, is there not a further and deeper stage in which one is unable to see anything at all?"

The Fourth Dimension
1924

I was recently informed by a lady that she had not only grasped the idea of the Fourth Dimension, but was able, in an hour of insight, to convey its meaning to an aged aunt. Alas! My friend cannot now remember the explanation. It really is tragic. The only person who could explain the Fourth Dimension has forgotten what it is!

Dodging
1925

"What sort of an actor is he?" asked one member of the dramatic profession of another. "Well," was the reply after a pause, "he is very good to his mother." That neat and kindly evasion reminded me of another case in which a literary man, referring to a deceased friend, observed, "He did not like Charles Dickens, but otherwise he was a good man."

Mortified
Estelle Roberts 1959

Countless numbers of people have come to me seeking evidence of survival. One woman, I recall, was shocked by the possibilities revealed by life after death. She was a prim, unmarried woman to whom I had said that I could see clairvoyantly three men around her. From my description, she identified them as her father and two brothers who had died. "They often come to see you at night after you've gone to bed," I told her. At this she sat bolt upright and said, "Mrs. Roberts, if Spiritualism teaches that male spirits can come into one's room after one has retired, I want nothing more to do with it!"

Letters to the Editor

Conspiracy Theory
1857

Modern history is replete with instances of blind bigotry exhibited by many most worthy and learned persons against the introduction of new inventions and improvements in society. Vaccination was denounced as the cruel despotic tyranny of forcing cow pox on the innocent babes of the poor, a gross violation of religion, morality, law, and humanity. The learned gravely print statements stating that vaccinated children became "ox-faced, that abscesses broke out to indicate sprouting horns, that the countenance was gradually transmuted into the visage of a cow, the voice into the bellowing of bulls, and that the character underwent strange mutations."

Inequities
1857

"It has been found necessary by the officers at the railroad depot in Asylum Street, to reduce the pay of the workmen on the wood trains by 20%. The labourers were offered 50 cents a day. A large force of them, Irishman all, refused to submit to the 20% off. The result was that, today, the wood train was made up entirely of Americans who have the good sense to take a job at half a dollar rather than do nothing."
The Hartford Times.

Editorial Comment: The above paragraph is running through the newspapers without a word of comment! It must be that people refuse the facts which it furnishes. Why cannot large railroad corporations begin their reductions, not with the poor labourers at the bottom rung of the ladder, but at the other end of the list? Is the meagre reduction of a few hundred men's low wages enough in amount to bring relief to the company? Any company practices the most refined cruelty when it cuts 20% from the wages of men who earn as little as these. Let them begin the reductions at the other end. Such a course as the above deserves no man's countenance or commendation.

A Royal Injustice
1858

Most Americans respect the lady who occupies the throne of great Britain [Queen Victoria], not for the diadem she wears, but for the qualities she possesses. Yet looking at the destitution which exists and spreads over the mining factories of England; thinking of the little children whose bodies and souls are crushed in the dungeons where the sun never enters, it is sad, very sad, to hear of titled rulers imposing such weary burdens upon the people.

The bells of London ring out joyously as each infant born of that Royal mother enters upon life; but down that dismal alley another mother clutches her infant - an infant with an immortal soul as perfect as the other - and moans for want of food to appease the hunger of her little one. Each prince or princess born in the palace snatches at the crust of bread the famished little one holds, in its bony fingers; binds to unrelenting toil the weary labourer; and forges another fetter for the aspiring mind.

It is time the people should arise. They too have a right to set their feet upon the Earth in freedom, and no more submit their life's best blood into sceptres for their rulers and manacles for themselves.

A Medium Replies
1858

Madam, I cannot satisfy you on the subject of Spiritualism. I can only advise you to satisfy yourself whether the mental phenomena are such as to indicate identities. This you can do by seeking the evidence. What is evidence to me cannot be evidence to you unless you see it and feel it. On this topic, man is so sceptical and so desirous of knowing the truth that, from his innermost soul, he rejects every evidence in which there is the least possible error. What one man may be satisfied with, another man is disposed to reject.

I may have felt that it would be a source of happiness to you at this time to know that your beloved still lives in all his attributes, in a condition not much different from that, which, in his happiest days, he knew here, merely divested of that cumbersome earthly frame that ties down the powers of man to a limited locality. Now, could you feel all this as a truth, how much happiness the conviction would give you. I hope you may realize it. But, alas! I am not able to do more than show you dimly the way. You must search for truth for yourself.

Reply to a Young Lady
1888

We would advise the young lady who asked about developing her mediumship to walk warily, and to use caution rather than giving way to impatience. The good or evil that she will get from mediumship depends largely on the methods by which she seeks its development. To most of us, the land of spirit is a *terra incognita*, and we embark on a journey attended with risk when we seek to penetrate it. We cross the frontier without a chart and, if we trust our development to accident, we may not fare so pleasantly.

As a rule, mediumship is best developed normally and not forced. It should grow spontaneously by patient waiting, regular sitting, and aspiration after that which is good. If it be impatiently forced, there is danger of disorderly development, false and misleading communications, bewilderment and pain. All depends on wisdom, caution, and the orderliness of the growth of those psychical faculties which, if left partially developed may, for that very reason, be a source of danger.

Spiritualists in a Box
1893

Not long ago, a letter was received in which this Editor was asked these two questions: "Are you really a Spiritualist?" and, "Were you *ever* a Spiritualist?" The Editor is accused of excluding subjects which the writers appear to think are connected with Spiritualism. Now, it should be perfectly understood that Spiritualism is a branch of study dealing with the unseen, and is neither synonymous with reincarnation, vegetarianism, anti-vivisectionism, anti-vaccinationism, or the eating of whole-meal bread. One may believe in the action of independent and unseen intelligences and study their modes of action, and still have a range of views about other matters as does the rest of the world. There should be no reason for the writer to blaspheme or, as is very often the case, to regard the word 'Spiritualist' as synonymous with the word 'crank'.

Silent Sympathy
1908

I have much sympathy with the man who violently rejected a piece of well-meant consolation proffered by a friend, who sought to raise his spirits by remarking in encouraging tones that, "the sun is shining somewhere!" "What's the use in that," answered the unfortunate one in a voice of disgust, "if it doesn't shine on me!" Not infrequently, the best and most tactful expression of sympathy is silence.

An English Vicar Resigns: The Price of Conscience
1912

Rev. Tom Primrose Castley has resigned his living near Stafford, and given his reasons in a letter to the parishioners, as follows:

> "I find it absolutely impossible to assent to many of those doctrines upon which the church has built. Religion and theology are two very different things. If the church orders me as one of her ministers to proclaim certain things as facts which I do not believe are facts, then the only thing is to give up my ministry. I cannot go on uttering in public what I cannot say privately. I cannot go on receiving the church's money under such circumstances. I cannot sacrifice my conscience for the sake of friends, money, or anything else. I had hoped to settle down in the parish on my own little farm, and to establish a co-operative among the small holders of the land, but this we could not do. So we joined the Small Holders Cooperative Colony of Norfolk where I hope to put into practice some of the principles I have always preached, and also add a little to our very small income."

The Bishop of Lichfield, accepting the resignation, says he deeply regrets the cause, but adds that he has no doubt the vicar is acting in all good conscience, whose dictates all must obey. He thanks the vicar for his past services.

Lion the Dog
1919

Mr. John tells of a dog named Lion. He belonged to a young Cambridge man to whom he was much attached, and for whom he reserved a special form of greeting. To others, he gave the customary doggie bark, but when his master called him he always replied with a peculiar joyous squeak. His master went to South Africa and died there, leaving his dog with his parents in England. On the night of his death, Lion was heard to 'squeak' as if in great excitement, at the very hour when his master passed away.

Later, the dog had a severe illness from which the best attention could not save him. This is how Mr. John describes his death: "In the middle of the night we were wakened by Lion giving the joyous squeak that he only used when answering Jack, and to our surprise, he was sitting up with a happy recognition in his bright eyes, which were fixed on the corner of the ceiling. He must have died in giving his answer to something he heard."

Queer? Yes, but then what know we of dogs? Or of death, for that matter?

Good Fortune
1921

I have quite a budget of stories of how visits to our Journal's offices have been immediately followed by a train of happy events. Well, it is a pleasant thing to hear, but I hope that it will not degenerate into a superstition of the mascot order. The best good fortune that can happen to anyone is the awakening of the sense of beauty, whether in nature or humanity.

Seeing the Aura
1921

Mr. H. W. Engholm tells us that when he was on a visit to New York some years ago, the fashionable cry was "How is your aura?" At the present time the subject of the aura is again prominent. The note of caution expressed by Sir Oliver Lodge in this issue will doubtless prompt some replies:

> "Would some observers - who state that without clairvoyance they can see an edging to the human body, try the same observation substituting for the patient a white or flesh-tinted plaster figure? My present impression is that what is perceived is a contrast or fatigue effect, explicable in terms of the retina."

A Curious Theory
1921

Sir Oliver Lodge suggests that a person with only an etheric body might have the power of borrowing a portion of matter and moulding it into recognisable shape; that human beings were 'materialisations' during life and that, if we can materialise for a certain span of years, why not for a few minutes? Not perfectly, perhaps, but, at any rate, it may be that they could borrow a portion of organised matter from certain people and use it even when they were on the other side, to make themselves visible enough to be photographed.

Unwise Yet Splendid
1923

Looking backward, I recall the lives of some of the old fighters whose valour and tenacity are beyond the possibility of true appreciation. Some of them gave not only their earthly fortunes to the cause, but lost their lives in service as they might have done on the battlefield. I recall some who spent their energies so lavishly that they laid waste their powers and their remaining days were bound in misery. It was not wise, of course, but it was splendid.

Patience
1932

Mrs. Emily Hinchcliffe, well known for her lectures describing the return of her husband, Captain Hinchcliffe, the airman who lost his life in an attempt to fly the Atlantic, is refreshingly outspoken in her comments on a certain class of Spiritualists who consult their spirit friends about every circumstance of daily life – "Even", as she says, "whether they should take an umbrella when they go out!" The rebuke is not unmerited, although we must be patient with those who, in psychic matters, are still in the infant class.

Community Calendar

In Peacetime

The Upcoming Season: Cassadaga Lake[30]
1891

Interest in these meetings has exceeded our expectations. W. J. Colville, a favourite author and teacher of Spiritual Science, will conduct a class in *Practical Metaphysics* and the *Theory and Practice of Spiritual Healing*. Every effort will be made to render the instruction useful to those who are seeking for knowledge and health. The Children's Lyceum will be made an attractive and beneficial adjunct, including a first-class teacher in elocution and physical culture who will give instruction to the children free of charge. Our programme of lecturers comprises some of the best talent in the land. Much attention is being given to the subject of *Political Equality*. Saturday August 15th is to be set apart as 'Women's Suffrage Day'. Susan B. Anthony of Rochester, N.Y.

---

[30] Later known as Lily Dale Assembly.

and Reverend Annie Shaw of Washington D.C. are to be the speakers.

Picnic at Bingley
1906

On Saturday the 31st, the friends at Bingley and district held a picnic and, the weather being fine, a large number attended and took part in the festivities. The place of resort was the Druids' Altar. The romantic scenery, bracing air, and sense of freedom combined to put the company in good humour. A few aged friends, whose hair had grown grey in the service of truth, were present and seemed to heartily enjoy the gambols of their younger brethren. Altogether, a pleasant time was spent, nothing occurring to mar the happiness of the company.

A Pleasant Afternoon
1916

The proceedings in the afternoon were devoted to clairvoyant descriptions by Mrs. Jamrach and Mrs. Cannock. These were of excellent evidential quality, names and messages being freely given. There were but two failures in the identifications of the many descriptions given, and those which were recognised were frequently of remarkable value as tests of the reality of the clairvoyant and clairaudient faculties employed, and elicited many tokens of admiration on the part of the audience. Alderman Davis gave the invocation, and Miss Edith Bolton sang with much feeling "The Gates of Mercy" and "Abide With Me."

Religious Discussions on Shipboard
Arthur Conan Doyle 1920

Sir A. Conan Doyle writes as follows from S.S. Naldera, August 25th: "It was stated yesterday that never since the P. & O. Company was founded has there been so much religious discussion upon a ship. Indeed, last night I addressed two hundred and eighty first-class passengers with Parsees, Mahomedans, Buddhists, and men of all persuasions, including the Christian Bishop of Kwang-Si, a most excellent prelate, far more human and broad minded and intelligent than most ecclesiastics. All went excellently. On Friday I am to address the second-class passengers in the Red Sea in August! - so I will have a warm time of it. But it is worth anything, for I find the whole world yearning for knowledge and not knowing how to get it, or how to distinguish the true from the false. We want more philosophy and fewer phenomena now, though the good medium is still the necessary starting point."

Canada, You Say?
1921
Canada appears to be taking an active interest in Spiritualism. The *Daily Graphic* writes: "It seems that in all sorts of places in Canada at this moment, it is not Kipling who is read but Conan Doyle and Oliver Lodge; in the case of Conan Doyle, not *Sherlock Holmes* but his works on Spiritualism; and in the case of Oliver Lodge, not his views on wireless telegraphy but *Raymond*."[31] This may be news to many people, but it does not surprise us.

Tea with Mrs. Annie Brittain
1921
Private Sittings Daily. Hours: 10 to 7
Seance: Monday next, 3 p.m. 2 shillings.
50, Westbourne Park Road, Bayswater, W.
Ladies only. Tea provided.

---

[31] Oliver Lodge's youngest son, Second Lieutenant Raymond Lodge, was killed in action in World War I. Lodge, Oliver J. (1916). *Raymond or Life and Death*. George H. Doran Company.

Poltergeists

1921

The *Boston Post* records strange phenomena happening at Konnebuk in connection with a girl, aged 14. It is stated that plaster is torn from the walls, furniture upset, locked doors opened, her clothing ripped, and other marvels occur. The father will not permit newspaper representatives to interview his daughter, and for talks on the affair with himself he makes a charge of ten dollars.

In Times of War

Clairvoyance & Psychometry

1916

Mr. Otto Von Bourg (the Swiss Psychic) will give a special series of séances, June 6th, 20th & 27th at 3 o'clock in the afternoon at the rooms of the London Spiritualist Alliance. These special circles are given by the medium to meet the demand for evidences chiefly in connection with those who are suffering in mind by reason of the present war. Admission: 1 shilling each person. 110 St. Martin's Lane, London, W.C.

Motor Ambulance Fund

J.J. Morse 1916

Having supplied five motor ambulance cars, and there being over £136 in hand, Mr. J.J. Morse, the treasurer of the fund which was initiated by the *Two Worlds Journal*, is appealing for the small balance of £52 to make up the sum required for another car. Donations may be addressed to him at 18 Corporation Street, Manchester. Cheques should be crossed: Motor Ambulance Account, Union Bank of Manchester, Corn Exchange Branch.

Church of Higher Mysticism
1917
22 Princes Street, Cavendish Square, W.
Sunday next: Morning service for our fallen heroes.
Evening: Mrs. Fairclough-Smith's trance address, "Our Spirit Homes".
Every Sunday night: Service of Intercession for our sailors and soldiers.

Reading in the Trenches
1919
Sir Arthur Conan Doyle informed us some time ago that the sales of his book, *The New Revelation*, exceeded those of his world-renowned *Sherlock Holmes* stories. During the war, too, a bookseller we know was kept busy supplying orders from soldiers in the trenches in France for *Raymond*, a large and costly book.

Mr. Frederick Brittain
1920
Magnetic, Mental or Absent Treatment. Boudoir Theatre, 12b Pembroke Gardens, Kensington. Every Tuesday and Friday morning. Free treatment for Soldiers suffering from nerve shock.

Curious Advertisements

---※-◦-◈---

Eno's Fruit Salt

Are you drawing an overdraft on the Bank of Life?
Late hours, fagged, unnatural excitement,
breathing impure air, too rich food,
alcoholic drink, gouty, rheumatic, blood poisons, biliousness,
headache, pimples on the face, lack of appetite? ENO'S
FRUIT SALT is an imperative hygienic need. It keeps
the blood pure, prevents fevers and bilious attacks, and
removes the injurious effects arising from stimulants and
narcotics such as alcohol, tobacco, tea and coffee.

"Yes, when I suffer from a brain overwrought,
Excited, feverish, worn from laboured thought,
Harassed by anxious care, or sudden grief,
I run to ENO and obtain relief."
Barrister-at-Law,
Whose years now number fourscore.

Wanted: Cripples!

Every cripple ought to know about the artificial
leg I make. I can save you half the price
and give you a better leg then you can get elsewhere.
Brothers, tell your cripple friends about this.
Write P. Williams, Salisbury, NC.

Planchette

Useful for developing the power of Automatic
Writing. Polished Mahogany board,
Brass fittings, Ivorine wheels, complete
in box with full instructions.

A Lady writes: "Your Planchette is beautifully
made and I am getting excellent results."
Home: 8 shillings post-free, Abroad: 9 shillings.
C. Manners-Smith, 26 Corporation Street, Manchester.

A Spiritualist Gentleman

A Spiritualist gentleman of many years' standing
desires admission to a serious circle.
Regular attendance promised. Accustomed
to sit in circle up to four years since.
C.S., 25 Moorgate Street, E.C. 2.

The New Reflectograph

Séances held with this instrument for the
purpose of spirit communication.
The Spirit Hand, fully materialized, may sometimes
be seen operating the Key Board in a good red light.
Private or group séances arranged by applying to the
Honourable Secretary, Miss R. Ermen, The Beacon,
102 Vineyard Hill Rd., Wimbledon Park, S.W. 19.

Spiritualists' Rest House

Brighton. For comfort, visit Temple House, 53 Marine
Parade. Facing SE and close to Palace Pier. Good table.
Expert chef. Late dinner. Vegetarians also catered for.
From 2½ guineas weekly.

Wanted: Caravan

Horse-drawn caravan for Healing Campaign Tour.
Will any kind sympathizer help this
advertiser to secure this, plus £100?
This will support him for 12 months. Highest credentials.

Responda: The Psychic Talking Card

The Psychic Talking Card and Pendulum for
messages and telepathic development.
An easy means of investigation into the psychic. Many who
earnestly desire communication and are making no progress
for want of an instrument. *Responda* is simple and sensitive
enough to yield results even to those endowed with but little
mediumship. Can be operated by one person sitting alone at
home. Miss J.U. Bexhill writes: "I am led to write and thank you
for the *Responda*. Words cannot express what it has already
done for me. I am in constant touch with
my dear father. Now I know."
Home, three shillings eight pence;
Abroad, four shillings, eight pence or $1.00.
R. A. Robson, 21 Fairfax Rd., Chiswick, London, W.4, England.

Character Delineation

Mrs. A. B. Severance respectfully announces
to the public that those who wish
may visit her in person, or send an autograph or lock of hair.
She will give an accurate description of their leading traits of
character and peculiarities of disposition, marked changes in
past and future life, physical disease with prescription therefor,
what business they are best adapted to pursue in order to
be successful, the physical and mental adaptation of those
intending marriage, and hints to the inharmoniously married.
Full delineation $2.00 and four, two-cent stamps.
Brief delineation $1.00 and four two-cent stamps.
1300 Main St., White Water, Walworth County, Wis.

Answers to Questions

*The following were given through the mediumship
of Mr. J.J. Morse, in reply to questions from
the audience during a sitting in 1927.*

*Question: "As a student of the philosophy of Andrew Jackson
Davis, I should be glad to learn whether his views can be regarded
as being in harmony with the general tenor of Spiritualistic teaching
in the present day?"*

Answer: "It must be remembered that no finality can be attached
to the writings, researches, or utterances of any psychical or
mediumistic person. Each and every statement must be judged
on its own merits in relation to the facts of Nature rather than as
the teachings of any particular school, or as being an expression
of all the truth on any given topic. Andrew Jackson Davis, for
example, would possibly modify some of his writings in the light
of later researches."

*Question: "Does not the happiness of the next life depend upon
the use we make of our opportunities in this?"*

Answer: "Undoubtedly the question states a truth, but to draw the
large inference that the whole of your future happiness depends
upon present conduct would be absolutely incorrect."

*Question: "Do those in spirit life require rest as we understand
the word?*

Answer: The reply was in the affirmative with a touch of characteristic humour. "Remember, if you please," he said, "that some of
you find it difficult to keep awake all night, and grumble desperately

when you are aroused from your beds in the morning. How would you find the prospect of having to keep awake forever?"

Question: "Are hereditary faculties confined only to the body, or are they spiritual in character?"

Answer: "Just as the hereditary transmission of bodily character exerts its influence on successive generations, so there *appears* to be a transmission of spiritual faculties; however, it is really an hereditary transmission of organic adaptability. This adaptability produces its impression on the astral or psychical body and the indwelling consciousness; and when it departs from its material surroundings, it finds in the astral or psychical body the condition or faculty that was so developed in the physical body. This distinction between material and psychical faculties is fallacious, for the astral or spiritual body, like its brother on the physical plane, is only an avenue through which is expressed the faculties of the indwelling consciousness. It is apparently so difficult for most people to realise that the bodily organisation as a whole is simply the vehicle through which are manifested the powers and qualities of the indwelling soul or consciousness. The essential point we wish to emphasise and place before you is that the physical and psychical bodies are avenues through which qualities are expressed, and not the originators of those qualities."

Question: "A man and woman are united in a harmonious and happy marriage, which is ended by the decease of one of them. The one who is left behind gets married again. Can Tien say if the second marriage is approved by the one in the spirit world? What will be the relation of the two to each other, joined as both were through mutual love with the third person?"

Answer: "If the inhabitants of the spirit world regarded the perplexities of existence in the same short-sighted way that mankind on the earth life regards them, unquestionably the great majority of second marriages would excite wrath, anger, and indignation on the other side. But we look at the thing from a very different point of view. Where two souls are bound together by the bonds of an indissoluble affection, though one may pass into the spirit life prior to the other, death has no power to dissolve that bond. And you must also understand, with regard to the contraction of second alliances, that a great number of marriages in human life are anything but of the character referred to in the question; there are marriages of convenience, marriages to gratify ambition, marriages to spite another. Now all these arise from the irregular and imperfect training and education of human beings in regard to this very serious - we had almost said holy - relationship. When the world is wiser and understands that such relationships must only rest on spiritual affinity and become marriages because it is in the nature of the parties, then all such questions will be disposed of."

Feature Column

————⟫-०-⟪————

Maria Hayden Brings Spiritualism to Europe & Great Britain

Being a narrative of the first visit of Maria Hayden to England, France, and Ireland, 1850-1853. Chronicled by her husband, Dr. William R. Hayden.

"We Meet Robert Owen"

The next distinguished inquirer was no less a personage than the venerable and renowned, Robert Owen, socialist and philanthropist. The first time he called on us, it was not for the purpose of investigating spiritual phenomena, but simply to purchase a copy of Mr. Ballou's book.

Mr. Owen was personally unknown to us at that time. As we stood by the fire talking of America, raps were heard upon the table which was at some distance from where we were then standing. So loud with the sounds as to attract the attention of Mr. Owen, although he was somewhat deaf. He inquired of Mrs. Hayden the meaning of the sounds, to which she replied that they were produced by spirits and that someone desired to communicate with him. "Very well", said the old gentleman, "if they have anything to say to me, let them say it, for I am always ready to hear all sides of a question."

Sitting himself at the table, he desired to know if anyone wished to communicate with him, to which he received an affirmative response together with the maiden name of his mother, Mary Williams. So far, so good; but a single test was far from being sufficient to satisfy a mind like Mr. Owen's. Proof followed proof, and séance followed séance, until there was no hinge upon which to hang a doubt. When once convinced of a fact, he was not the man to let his light be hidden under a bushel, and the result of his investigations was the appearance of his celebrated *Manifesto*.

The *Manifesto* fell like a thunderbolt upon the religious world. To them, this great pillar and giant had fallen! The most mortifying part was that he had been converted by the vile 'Spirit Rappers' and not by the Clergy. The celebrated Bishop of Durham stated that, "a monument ought to be erected to Mrs. Hayden for having made a Christian of the infidel, Robert Owen."

Would to God that the celebrated Bishop was a thousandth part the Christian that the despised Robert Owen is. If the noble Bishop followed half so closely in the footsteps of his Divine Master as does Robert Owen, there would not be so many starving, dying, and ignorant poor in that great capital of wealth and poverty; he would not require 80,000 pounds per annum to support his extravagance, keep his carriages, his brood, and yelping bloodhounds, while many poor clergyman almost starve for want of sufficient bread to support themselves. Mr. Robert Owen does not simply preach but he does a thousand times more - he practises what he preaches.

By invitation of Mr. Owen, we dined with him on his 82nd birthday. He was in the best of spirits with a mind as clear and lucid as a man of forty. He spoke of his eventful life, remarking that he had done nothing that he regretted or would wish undone. His whole aim had been to improve the condition of his fellow men. Until the moment he came out against the clergy, he had been one of the most popular men in Europe; but he felt it his duty to oppose priestcraft and he did so, well knowing what the consequences would be to himself.

In conclusion, I will relate an anecdote as it is characteristic of the man. One morning, as I sat reading a scurrilous attack upon us in one of the papers, Mr. Owen entered and I complained to him of the unfairness and falsehood of the writer, naturally expecting sympathy. But to my astonishment he clapped his hands together in great glee, exclaiming, "I am glad of it! And I hope they will continue to come out against you, stronger and stronger every day!" This was anything but consoling to my own mind, and I asked him if he would be so kind as to explain. "Explain? Explain?" said Mr. Owen, "Why they are splendid advertisements at no cost. You are bound to thank them for their efforts on your behalf. Opposition is the life of all progress. It has done me more good than all the praise in the world." Such were the words of wisdom from a sage philosopher, as I afterwards learned to regard him.

"We Receive a Public Letter from Dr. John A. Ashburner[32]"

My dear Mr. Hayden,

You perceive, from the kind of notice in *The Leader*, that you have here in Britain no chance for fair or candid examination of the phenomena you have crossed the Atlantic to lay before the public. You must not expect high-minded conduct from the press.

You have, in this country, a high mission. Pay no attention to the absurd insinuation respecting money. You must take money unless you can manage to live without it. I do not believe that our countrymen worship mammon less fervently than the inhabitants of Yankee-land! It is your mission to introduce a knowledge which shall, in due time, inevitably lead to the destruction of intolerance which distinguishes the bigot of every creed.

There are many desirous of investigating your phenomena who are barred from doing so by having placed their minds under the influence of frivolous sceptics, or by approaching the subject in a less-than-humble frame of mind. To those who quietly, patiently, and with due humility come to the study of these manifestations, I can promise a treat which is equalled only by that peace of mind which passeth understanding.

I remain, my dear Mr. Hayden,

Yours, very truly,

John Ashburner

30th March, 1853.

---

[32] Dr. John A. Ashburner (1793-1853) Royal College of Surgeons. Physician to the Small-pox hospital, London, and Queen Charlotte's Lying In Hospital, London. Lecturer of Midwifery and the Diseases of Women and Children at St. Thomas' Hospital.

"Two Curious Incidents"

We had not been in England more than a few months before two or three persons were advertising themselves as mediums. Among these was a Mr. and Mrs. Roberts who announced themselves as "the celebrated American mediums"; that they were prepared to "gratify serious and enlightened minds with spirit communications from their departed friends."

We feel impressed to give it as our humble opinion that they were deeply imbued with the spirit of fanaticism, and did much to bring the phenomena into disrepute in London during the short time in which they continued to "gratify serious, and enlightened minds." Instead of being Americans, they were both Irish (as they afterwards testified under oath) and with the richest kind of brogue! Being unable to pay their way, they then left London for Cheltenham, taking with them an insane mesmeric subject named Julius. Arraying himself in scarlet robes and haranguing people in the street, he was taken in charge by the police. Shortly afterwards, in company with Mr. & Mrs. Roberts, they set sail for the United States since which time we have not heard of their whereabouts.

On another occasion, picking up the *London Times*, we were somewhat surprised and indignant to read an advertisement informing the "Curious Public" that Mrs. Hayden would obtain communications from the spirits of the departed upon the receipt of half a crown, to be enclosed to Mrs. Hayden and deposited at the store of a respectable tradesmen in

Pall Mall! Suffice it to say, that some unprincipled person had taken the liberty of borrowing Mrs. Hayden's name and popularity for the purpose of defrauding the 'curious public'.

We immediately paid a visit to the place designated by the said "Mrs. Hayden" but surprisingly - she was not at home.

A Parting Thought

Death has no power the immortal soul to slay,
That, when its present body turns to clay,
Seeks a fresh home, and with un'minished might
Inspires another flame with life and light.

Pythagoras[33]

---

[33] Found in: Diogenes Laertius. (c. AD 300). *Lives of the Eminent Philosophers.* Oxford University Press, 2018.

"Truth is a silent knowing."

Coral Polge

Vocatus Atque Non Vocatus, Deus Aderit.

About Debra Skelton

Debra teaches *Sacred Gesture, Voice of the Medium,* and *Sacred Theatre for the Sensitive* at the Inner Quest Foundation, specializing in the somatic experience via embodied movement for the developing sensitive. She holds a BFA (Theatre) from the University of Alberta, and is a creative link to the oral tradition of legendary theatre innovator, Etienne Decroux. Debra is currently a teacher, healer and course organizer at the Inner Quest Centre, and author of *Echoes: Teachings from the Past, Wisdom for the Present.*

About The Inner Quest

The Inner Quest is a Centre for Integrated Awareness dedicated to the ethical holistic development of practitioners of the esoteric arts. Its purpose is to facilitate an awareness of our natural spiritual foundations within the practices of mediumship, healing, personal transformation, and many of the lesser known aspects of the esoteric experience.

The Inner Quest provides an ongoing program of classical study for the serious student and has established an international reputation for developing sound spiritual practitioners while reigniting the intrinsically sacred nature of the intuitive arts. Based in Victoria, Canada, it also houses the Open Door Sanctuary and the Inner Quest Press, publishers of *Magician to Mystic: A Mediumistic Path to a Spiritual Life* by Brian S. Robertson and Simon G. James, and *Echoes: Teachings from the Past, Wisdom for the Present* by Debra Skelton.

We invite you to discover more about the programs and courses offered by the Inner Quest Foundation and the IQ Sophia Community by visiting www.innerquestfoundation.com.

References

Anonymous. (1857). *How the Thing is to be Done*. Banner of Light Weekly Journal.

Baxter, J. Frank. (1891). *Has Spiritualism Anything to Do with National Ethics?* Lecture given at Onset Bay, Maine, August, 1891.

Bekoff, Marc. (2000). *Redecorating Nature: Deep Science, Holism, Feeling, and Heart*. BioScience, Oxford University Press.

Blavatsky, Helena P. (1888). *The Secret Doctrine*. Theosophical University Press.

Bohm, David. (1993). *Science, Spirituality, and the Present World Crisis*. ReVision: A Journal of Consciousness and Transformation, Heldref Publications.

Brigham, Helen Temple. (1920). *Inspirational Prayer: Address and Poems*. Privately published pamphlet.

Britten, Emma Hardinge. (1875). *Art Magic*. Progressive Thinker Publishing House.

Burnside, Thomas. (1880). Untitled. Herald of Progress Weekly Journal.

Caird, John. (1880). *An Introduction to the Philosophy of Religion*. Found in "Varieties of Religious Experience" by William James, 1902.

Calder, Alexander. (1878.) *Meditation and the Voice of Conscience*. Found in "Rifts in the Veil" published by W. H. Harrison, 1878.

Crookes, William. (1926). *Researches in the Phenomena of Spiritualism*. The Two Worlds Publishing Company, Ltd.

Daniels, Michael. (2005). *Shadow, Self, Spirit: Essays in Transpersonal Psychology*. Imprint Academic.

Davis, Andrew Jackson. (1850). *The Philosophy of Special Providences: A Vision*. William White and Company.

Davis, Andrew Jackson. (1860). *Individual Freedom*. Fourth Annual Spiritual Register. Spiritual Clarion Newspaper.

Davis, Andrew Jackson. (1893). *The Children's Progressive Lyceum*. Colby and Rich, Banner Publishing House.

Denslow, Van Buren. (1878). *The Influence of Religious Enthusiasm over Morals*. The Spiritualist Newspaper.

Doyle, Arthur Conan. (1918). *The New Revelation*. Hodder and Stoughton.

Doyle, Arthur Conan. (1920). *Religious Discussions on Shipboard*. Light: A Journal of Psychical, Occult, and Mystical Research. The Spiritual Alliance.

Drummond, Henry. (1888). *Natural Law in the Spirit World*. Hodder and Stoughton.

Einstein, Albert. (1930). *Religion and Science*. Found in "Ideas and Opinions", Three Rivers Press, 1954. Originally published in the New York Times Magazine, 1930.

Einstein, Albert. (1931). *The World as I See It*. Found in "Ideas and Opinions", Three Rivers Press, 1954. Originally published in "Living Philosophies", Simon and Shuster, 1931.

Einstein, Albert. (1934). *The Religious Spirit of Science*. Found in "Ideas and Opinions", Three Rivers Press. Originally published in "Mein Weltbild", Amsterdam: Querido Verlag, 1934.

Einstein, Albert. (1940). *On Freedom*. Published in "Freedom: Its Meaning" by Ruth Anshen. Routledge.

Einstein, Albert. (1948). *A Message to Intellectuals*. Letter addressed to the World Congress of Intellectuals in Defence of Peace. Bulletin of the Atomic Scientists: Science and Public Affairs.

Einstein, Albert. (1954). *Human Rights*. Address to Chicago Decalogue Society. New York Times.

Garrett, Eileen. (1943). *Awareness*. Berkley Publishing Company.

Garrett, Eileen. (1950). *The Sense and Nonsense of Prophecy*. Berkley Publishing Company.

Gibbes, E. B. (1937). *Controls as Separate Entities*. Psychic Science: Quarterly Transactions of the British College of Psychic Science, Ltd.

Hartelius, G., Rothe, G., & Roy, P. (2013). *Brand for the Burning*. In H. L. Friedman & G. Hartelius (Eds.), The Wiley-Blackwell Handbook of Transpersonal Psychology, Wiley Blackwell.

Hastings, Arthur. (2002). *The Resistance to Belief*. Journal of Near-Death Studies. Human Sciences Press, Inc.

Hatton, Eric. (2010). *Taking Up the Challenge*. Saturday Night Press Publications.

Hayden, William R. (1857). *Seven Years with the Spirits in the Old and New World*. Banner of Light Weekly Journal.

Hill, J. Arthur. (1918). *Man is a Spirit*. Cassell and Company, Ltd.

Hillman, James. (1989). *A Blue Fire*. Harper and Row.

Holmes, Ernest S. (1934). *The Ebell Lectures on Spiritual Science*. DeVorss & Co.

Hopps, John Page. (1870). *The Legal Status of Spiritualism*. Harbinger of Light Monthly Journal.

Hopps, John Page. (1873). *Lunacy at Work*. The Truthseeker Weekly Journal.

Hyslop, James H. (1900). *Two Separate Problems in Psychic Research*. Journal of the American Society for Psychical Research.

James, Simon G. (2022). *The Mediumistic Experience as Living Myth: A Search for Meaning*. MSc thesis in Consciousness, Spirituality and Transpersonal Psychology. Liverpool John Moores University.

James, William. (1896). *The Will to Believe*. An Address to the Philosophical Clubs of Yale and Brown Universities. New World Journal.

James, William. (1902). *The Varieties of Religious Experience.* Longmans, Green & Co.

Jung, Carl G. (1965). *Memories, Dreams, Reflections.* Vintage Books.

Kimmerer, Robin Wall. (2013). *Braiding Sweetgrass.* Milkweed Editions.

Knox, Howard J. (1914). *The Philosophy of William James.* Constable and Company.

Lancaster, Brian L. (2004). *Approaches to Consciousness: The Marriage of Science and Mysticism.* Red Globe Press.

Leonard, Gladys Osborne. (1937). *The Last Crossing.* Cassell and Company Ltd.

Lodge, Oliver. (1870). *Reason and Belief.* Methuen and Company, Ltd.

Lowe, Louisa. (1877). *The Ends, Aims, and Uses of Modern Spiritualism.* Paper read at the Annual Conference of the British National Association of Spiritualists, February, 1877.

Patten, Terry. (2018). *A New Republic of the Heart.* North Atlantic Books.

Polge, Coral. (1991). *Living Images: The Story of a Psychic Artist.* Regency Press.

Ravindra, Ravi. (1995). *Science and the Sacred.* Lecture given at the International Conference on the Unity of the Sciences.

Roberts, Estelle. (1959). *Estelle Roberts: Fifty Years a Medium.* Reprint published by Inner Quest Press, 2010.

Robertson, Brian S. (2022). *The Medium and Community: The Medium's Experience in an Esoteric Online Community of Integrative Transpersonal Practice.* MSc thesis in Consciousness, Spirituality and Transpersonal Psychology. Liverpool John Moores University.

Robertson, Brian S. & James, Simon G. (2017). *Magician to Mystic: A Mediumistic Path to a Spiritual Life.* Inner Quest Press.

Robinson, Oliver. (2017). *Paths Between Head and Heart.* John Hunt Publishing Ltd.

Skelton, Debra. (2017). *Echoes: Teachings from the Past, Wisdom for the Present*. Inner Quest Press.

Twigg, Ena. (1973). *Ena Twigg: Medium*. W. H. Allen and Co. Ltd.

Upham, Charles W. (1857). *Wise Conclusion*. Banner of Light Weekly Journal.

Vay, Baroness Adelma. (c.1878). *Fashionable Grief for the Departed*. Found in "Rifts in the Veil" by W. H. Harrison, 1878.

Wallace, Alfred R. (1870). *A Defence of Modern Spiritualism*. The Fortnightly Review.

Wallace, Alfred R. (1870). *Immortality*. Found in "Rifts in the Veil" published by W. H. Harrison, 1878.

Woollam, Ray H. (1989). *Have a Plain Day*. Unica Publishing.